Essentially
CANDLES

The Elegant Art of Candle Making
& Embellishing

Dr. Robert S. McDaniel & Katherine J. McDaniel

700 East State Street • Iola, WI 54990-0001
715/445-2214 • FAX: 715/445-4087   www.krause.com

Please call or write for our free catalog of publications. Our toll-free number to place an order or obtain a free catalog is 800-258-0929 or please use our regular business telephone 715-445-2214.

All photography by Dr. Robert S. McDaniel and Katherine J. McDaniel or Krause Publications.

Library of Congress Cataloging-In-Publication Data

ISBN: 0-87341-996-0
LC: 2001088599

Printed in the United States of America

$\mathcal{A}$CKNOWLEDGMENTS

We gratefully wish to thank the many people in the candle and fragrance industries who have helped our task by generously providing technical expertise, information, supplies, and encouragement. Special thanks go to Bill Binder at Candlewic for his technical insights as well as abundant material assistance; Helmut Gutberlet at Schuemann Sasol; Ricky Boscarino at Luna Parc for his custom-made candle holders; Carol K. Russell; Mike Lawson at Columbus Foods; Bob Kauffmann at the RIT® dye division of Best Foods®; John Harrell at Aroma Tech; and our continued love and devotion to Our Lady of Fatima.

$\mathcal{T}$ABLE OF CONTENTS

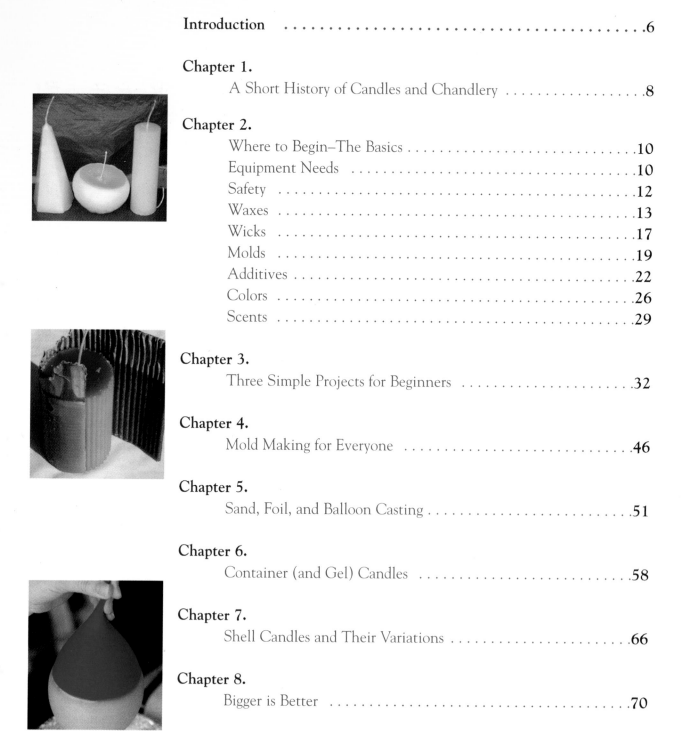

INTRODUCTION

"It's better to light one candle, than to curse the darkness."
Motto of The Christophers

A candle flame.

Technically, a candle is a combustion "engine" delivering fuel to and maintaining a heat source leading to the production of light and heat. Specifically, igniting a *wick* produces heat that in turn melts the surrounding wax. The molten wax flows to the wick and is carried to the flame by capillary action—the same forces that "wick" water into a paper towel or pull a drop of coffee into a sugar cube.

While the heat from the flame is sufficient to progressively melt the surrounding wax, it is not sufficient to set it aflame. As the wax ascends the wick, the flame progressively heats it until it vaporizes in the dark core of the flame. The wax begins to decompose into simpler compounds in the bright center of the flame (the so-called reducing zone). Finally, in the outermost zone, the wax reaches combustion temperature, combining with oxygen from the air, producing heat (plus water and carbon dioxide), and continuing the cycle.

This elegant description of a burning candle is condensed and adapted from a series of lectures by the great chemist Michael Faraday, presented in 1860!

Problems can occur if the candle is not designed properly. If the candle is colored by pigmentation rather than wax-soluble dyes, the pigments tend to clog the wick, diminishing or eliminating the capillary action required to deliver the molten fuel to the flame. If the wick is too large for the wax supply, it supplies an excess of wax to the flame, leading to the production of smoke—just as a car engine burning a too-rich fuel mixture produces smoke. When the wick is too small for the candle, it does not melt the entire wax pool, and the candle will burn down the center, leaving an unburned shell behind. Finally, if the wax forms an overly-large crystal structure, the candle will appear blotchy and irregular.

A well-designed candle requires the right wax for the application, together with the correct wick. *Container candles* require a low-melting wax, so that the entire contents of the container melt. They also need a *tabbed* wick with a metal core, so that the wick does not topple over during use. Dipped *tapers* require a sticky wax composition to allow the layers to build up, forming the tapered column. Molded candles need a non-sticky wax composition (to enable removal from the mold) with a wick shape and size appropriate to the diameter of the candle; and the wax needs to be hard enough to resist softening in hot weather.

Today's candles are used more for mood and romance than for light. Artistic considerations have led to the development of a number of additives to help the modern chandler create candle art that appeals to many senses. There is a specific amount of fragrance material that the molten candle wax can dissolve and then retain in the solid state. Branched *polymers* are often added to *paraffin* to disrupt the internal order. This allows the paraffin to dissolve more *fragrance oils*.

Moreover, branched polymers also affect the *viscosity* (thickness) of the molten wax, often causing the candle to burn longer.

There is a wide range of modern additives to choose from to enhance the overall effects designed into a candle. Additives are available to:

- Produce a more opaque or translucent candle
- Produce more vivid colors
- Produce or eliminate mottled effects
- Prevent colors from fading in the daylight
- Reduce stickiness

But the best additives are still human creativity and imagination. The function, beauty, and overall effect are up to the chandler's skill, not the availability of high tech ingredients. Within the pages of this book, it is our wish to provide our readers with a guide to candlemaking that will help all of them, from those who have an annual candlemaking project to those who are trying to carve their niche in the business world with a cottage industry.

For large-scale production, there are great devices that let you handle wax safely, even in bulk. Although the equipment depicted herein will seem like a ragtag assortment of cans and hotplates—they often are—please realize that the best equipment for the job is the right size, economical for the user, easy to use, and clean.

For the beginner and small candlemaker, we recommend the sort of equipment found within these pages. But we are certainly aware that personal deep fryers, crock pots, and related equipment are more suited to the individual making dozens of candles, and that large wax melters and banks of *molds* are ideal for large production runs. We are mostly concerned with the techniques and raw materials for candles, rather than thousands of dollars of fancy equipment.

CHAPTER 1
A Short History of Candles and Chandlery

When all candles be out, all cats be gray.

English proverb

Man has long been fascinated by and dependent on fire. The light and heat of fire was one of man's earliest treasures. It was carried from place to place as clans moved with the beasts they hunted, and it was zealously maintained in the primitive hearths of those who gathered and foraged. With the knowledge and control of fire, man turned night into day and became a tool wielder, dreamer, and generalist, holding the beasts at bay.

Fire has always been considered a gift of the gods, though not necessarily a willingly given one. Prometheus, serving the forges of the gods, stole fire and gave it to man. He was chained to a mountain peak under continuous torture for his actions. In a different myth, it was the noble wolf that stole the divine fire and brought it to man as a gift. Every culture has its own myth that recounts man's mastery of fire.

Man quickly learned what burned and what did not. A burning brand could easily be taken from the fire to dispel, at least briefly, the darkness. Dried reeds could be thrust into the fire as a more portable and quickly lit, though transient, torch. The cave paintings around Lascaux, France, painted some 15,000 years ago, were made by

Of course candles are known for their ambiance rather than their chemistry. A simple lantern reflects the candle flame over and over.

the light of stone lamps with "wicks" of moss that burned fat. Perhaps 10,000 years later, the Egyptians made candles of beeswax, using a section of reed as a wick, and also used "rush lights" (reed sections soaked in molten tallow).

The Romans are credited with making the next major advance in candle construction. They used fibers of flax, hemp, or cotton as wicks in pots filled with tallow or pitch. Or they dipped the wicks repeatedly into molten tallow to build up a candle.

Western civilization was not alone in developing candles. Cinnamon was boiled in India to isolate a functional and fragrant wax; and the Japanese isolated a waxy insect exude found in trees for their lamps and candles.

Because of cost and availability, tallow from sheep, goats, cattle, or oxen was the normal fuel source. Beeswax was priced out of reach of the common man, available only to the rich or to the church. Because of the rich, uplifting scent of the burning beeswax, the church considered it a gift from God for the spiritual benefit of man. This stood in direct contrast to the effects of tallow-based candles, which emitted a black, sooty smoke and thick, acrid odor.

Nonetheless, even tallow candles were often beyond the reach of the general population, due to the scarcity of meat in their diet. They often had to rely on dried, resinous splinters of wood for light.

In England, chandlers (candlemakers) plied their trade door-to-door. The English tallow Chandlers Guild was incorporated and started to control the candle trade in 1462; and the "higher class" Wax Chandlers Guild was founded in 1484. At about the same time, molds for candles first appeared in Paris.

Candle technology was both controlled and static until the late 18th and 19th centuries, when candles and candlemaking reached their zenith and then almost disappeared. In the 18th century, whaling became a lucrative industry, harvesting oil and spermaceti wax for lamps and candles. Spermaceti, found in the head cavities of the sperm whale, was hard enough to resist the heat of summer (which caused most candles to soften, bend, and distort) and burned with a clean, bright flame. In fact, spermaceti candles were so good and in such demand that candlepower came to be defined as the amount of light emitted by a 1/6-pound pure spermaceti candle burning at a rate of 120 grams per hour.

Early in the 19th century, the scientific work of Chevreul, the original fat chemist, began to elucidate the chemical nature of tallow and led to the production of stearin and stearic acid (in ca. 1825). Stearic acid found use, added to wax, as a hardener, opacifier, and mold release. With the invention of the braided wick, also in 1825, the stage was set for the invention of a continuous candlemaking machine that came in 1834, the same year that mordanted wicks were introduced.

The discovery of petroleum in Pennsylvania in the early 1800s led to the commercial production of paraffin (a residue from oil distillation) by the 1850s. Paraffin, though soft, burned cleanly, brightly, and without odor. Blending the soft paraffin with stearic acid as a hardener, gave a superior and cheaper candle—unfortunately not soon enough to safeguard the over-fished sperm whale population. Nevertheless, this dramatic improvement in candle technology also led to the decline of candle usage, since kerosene (from petroleum) burned in lamps became the common source of illumination. Kerosene was later displaced by the light bulb, first introduced in 1879.

Since 1900, candles have frequently enjoyed periodic resurgences in popularity, driven now by artistry and romance, fragrance and aromatherapy. And it is still hard to provide more delight to a child than the favorite camp torch—a flaming marshmallow on a stick. Light, heat, sweet fragrance, and deliciously edible; no child would ask for more.

Flowers and candles can set a mood without words.

CHAPTER 2
Where to Begin–The Basics

The best candle is understanding.
Welsh proverb

The basic equipment needed is:

* A pot for boiling water
* Wicking
* Wax
* Thermometer
* Container in which you melt the wax
* A mold—the molds can be as simple as a frozen orange juice can or a homemade mold, made from corrugated paper. In fact, if you want to concentrate on hand-dipped tapers, you don't even need a mold.

Equipment Needs

You don't need a lot of expensive equipment to make candles, though you can spend a lot of money along the line, depending on what (and how many) you want to make. There are roughly four levels of equipment available to the candlemaker.

Basic equipment shown includes a scale and wax thermometer. Although wax can be melted as shown, directly on the heat element, this is usually only done for high melting additives. A hot water bath, double boiler, or jacketed system such as a Crock-Pot® or deep fryer are more typically and more safely used.

Minimum equipment for a beginner includes a hot plate, thermometer, simple wax, hot water bath, wicks, and cans for simple molds.

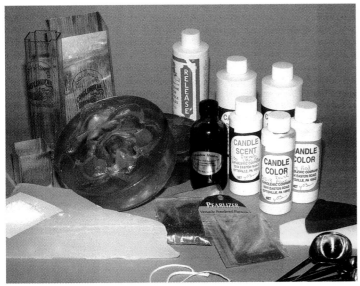

Candlemakers often start out with just a few molds, colors, and fragrances.

As the candlemaker's ambition grows, so does the collection of molds and additives.

After these basic needs are met, you might add candle dyes and fragrances, stearic acid, a set of measuring spoons, and perhaps a commercial mold or two to get to the next level. Some mold-release spray may also be needed, depending on the type of wax and mold you are using. Depending on how many candles you intend to make and how many colors and fragrances you want on hand, your total investment at this point could be as little as $50 or as much as $200 and up.

The third level is that of the burgeoning professional or very serious hobbyist who will add a collection of different types, shapes, and sizes of molds along with a scale, various chemical additives to alter and enhance appearance, and different types of waxes and wicks for special candles—in general more of everything. At this level your investment will probably start at $200-$300 and can go much higher,

depending on the number and types of molds you invest in. The good news is that you are now probably buying your wax in bulk, so the cost of each candle is reduced drastically.

The final level of involvement means scaling up to production with large, temperature-controlled melting vats, banks of molds, dye concentrates, and larger volumes of fragrance components.

In addition to these needs, or wants, we would also add a diary or journal. Although it is often overlooked, keeping a written record of your work will help you to determine what works and what does not. It will enable you to identify what made interesting candles and how to reproduce the effects. It will also facilitate experimentation by allowing you to make incremental changes to a starting recipe. In short, a journal is a good investment at almost any level.

Safety

Paraffin is a moderately low-melting solid that will not dissolve in water. Since it is organic, it is combustible, especially in the hot, melted state. This is essential to its performance in a candle, but it is also a hazard, since we have to melt the various waxes in order to make candles.

Flash point is the lowest temperature where vapors will sustain combustion (remain lit) when ignited. For paraffins, this temperature is roughly 406 F (208 C). Typical handling temperatures for molten wax are on the order of 140-200 F (60-93 C), so the major safety threat at these temperatures is the possibility of inadvertent skin contact causing burns. This is a particular problem since wax is insoluble in water and thus cannot be easily washed off. You usually have to pick it off once it has cooled enough to solidify.

When the vapor from molten wax is exposed to heating elements (gas fires, electric burners, etc.), there is a danger of the wax catching fire. Heating elements attain temperatures well above the flash point and often above the *auto-ignition point* of waxes (482-617 F, 250-325 C). For this reason, it is a good idea to use indirect heat (a double boiler, or a hot water bath) rather than heating a container of wax directly on a heating element. Although direct heating of wax may be necessary to dissolve some high melting additives, this should always be done carefully and using the smallest amounts of wax possible. Avoid red-hot electric elements and high, gas flames.

It is a good idea to have a small, multiply rated fire extinguisher on hand when melting wax. You can usually contact your local fire department for instructions on the right way to use a fire extinguisher. If a fire extinguisher is not available, common household ingredients such as salt and baking soda may be used to smother small, contained fires. Remember that fire extinguishers are only meant to put out small, contained fires or to help you get to an exit. Your first obligation in any fire situation is to get yourself and others to safety.

Fire extinguisher and hot plate. Safety should always be of primary concern. A hot plate enables the candles to be prepared away from other flammable materials.

When making a container candle, use containers that have been made for candles; ordinary glass may break from thermal shock due to the flame and hot wax. If you are making candles for gifts or for resale, include safe-use instructions in the package. Protect your friends and customers as well as yourself.

Never leave melting or molten wax unattended. Never leave a burning candle unattended. When burning a candle, be sure that no flammable objects (drapes, lampshades, etc.) are above or nearly above the candle. Keep burning candles out of the reach of children and pets.

To remove wax drips, you should usually allow the wax to cool (and can sometimes use ice cubes to hasten this process). Then pick off as much wax as possible. Residual wax can often be removed from fabric by placing an absorptive material or fabric on top of the residual wax and then running an iron, on low heat, over the fabric-covered drip. This will melt the wax, which will then transfer to the more absorptive fabric.

Waxes

In 1995 there were approximately 1.3 billion pounds of petroleum waxes produced or imported into the United States. (And retail sales of candles, not counting accessories, are in excess of $2 billion annually!)

A wax is an easily melted, organic material that is plastic or malleable in the solid state, deforming easily under pressure. (That means you can roll it out.) Today the dominant types of wax used in candles, at least in North America, are paraffin and beeswax (available at craft stores, candle suppliers, or local beekeepers). Paraffin waxes are polymers obtained from the purification of various petroleum fractions (usually containing between 20 and 36 carbon atoms) during the refining process. Beeswax and many vegetable waxes are high molecular weight esters–the condensation products of fatty acids and fatty alcohols.

Whatever their source, candle waxes are characterized by such properties as *melting point*, *melt viscosity*, hardness (measured by *needle penetration*), stickiness, crystal size, flexibility, and the ability to retain oils within their crystalline matrix. It is a mistake to try to characterize waxes solely by their melting point, since beeswax is very sticky but high melting, while carnauba is hard, non-sticky, and even higher melting. *Microcrystalline waxes*, on the other hand, have very small, flexible crystals and a wide range of melting points. They retain oils well, but range from tacky to hard and brittle. The selection of wax is often a difficult task to the novice.

Paraffin wax is produced from petroleum distillation and comes in a variety of melting points, 120-170 F (49-77 C). It was once believed that the melting point was dependent on the amount of residual oil in the paraffin, but that's not true. The melting point is determined solely by the molecular weight and type of hydrocarbon chains in the wax, though commercially blended formulations occasionally have added oil to decrease the melting point, or they have hardeners such as stearic acid to raise the melting point. In general, it is undesirable to use oil to reduce the melting point, since paraffin has limited ability to retain oil (usually 1.5-2% of the candle's weight), and any added oil will further limit the ability to add fragrance without producing mottling or worse—oil exuding to the surface.

There is quite a bit of overlap as to uses for the various melting range waxes, since it is relatively easy to raise or lower the melting point through additives. In general, low melting points are desirable for container candles, because the entire contents of the container are meant to be burned. High melting point waxes are used for long-burning candles and for wax shells that are designed to be used with *votives* or small taper inserts (*hurricanes*). High melting point waxes can also be used for *overdipping* tapers and pillars. Medium melting waxes, roughly 130-140 F melting points, are most often used for general candlemaking, since they can be adjusted as desired. Mineral oil, *petroleum jelly*, or even vegetable shortening can be added to lower the melting point, or stearic acid and *polyethylene* can be added to raise the melting point.

- 125-128 F wax: These soft waxes are normally used for container candle fill, blending with harder waxes, or for hand-forming decorative pieces. They are also used for making wax hands by dipping a moist hand into a carefully temperature-controlled bath or wax.

- 135 F wax: Often used for tapers, blending, or for hand-forming decorative pieces.

- 145 F wax: This is a good general-purpose candle wax for pillars and sand-cast candles. It gives a smooth, hard finish and does well in hot weather.

- 155 F wax: This is a hard wax often used for glazing and overdipping. It has some tendency to fracture.

- 165 F wax: Mostly used for blending to increase the hardness of softer, lower melting waxes.

Paraffin wax is usually found as 11-pound slabs or as a case of four to five slabs. However, it is also available as beads, flakes, and similar small forms. Paraffin from the grocery store shelf comes in one-pound boxes (four 1/4-pound slices) and usually represents a 135 F wax.

Spermaceti wax is obtained from the head cavity of the sperm whale. Spermaceti was once the candle wax of choice due to its hardness as well as the bright and clean burning nature of the flame. But today whales are mostly protected in an effort to prevent their extinction. Synthetic spermaceti (melting point 131-133 F, 55-56 C) is now available, but has mostly been replaced in candles by paraffin waxes plus various additives.

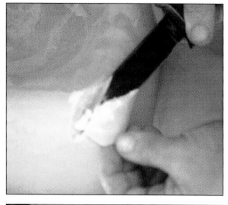

Beeswax, even in a large 11-pound block, is soft. It will not shatter, so it must be cut with a chisel or similar instrument. We use a screwdriver and/or an old bayonet.

Honey being delivered into a heated vat.

Beeswax production at the Swenson Apiary in rural Minnesota. Honeycomb from a hive is placed on a production line.

Crude molten beeswax.

Capping. The beeswax top surface is opened.

Waste produced by preliminary refining of beeswax.

The comb is opened by machine to allow extraction of honey

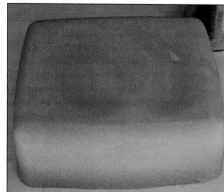

A large block of semi-refined beeswax.

Beeswax, exuded from the body of the industrious honeybee, is a complex mixture of hydrocarbons, wax esters, propolis (the glue that sticks the comb to the hive), and traces of honey and other materials. Crude beeswax is usually a dark tan (refined, it is a golden color) melting at about 143.6-149 F (62–65 C).

Although beeswax is higher melting and cleaner burning than tallow, it is extremely sticky and at one time could only be used in hand-dipped tapers. However, modern polyurethane or silicone rubber molds and silicone spray release agents allow the production of 100% beeswax molded candles. (We recently made a 3" X 36" bleached beeswax Paschal candle in an acrylic mold, with a removable polyurethane base, without any additives at all—unless you count worry as an additive.) Beeswax, poured at 170-180 F (77 to 82 C) also tends to exhibit low shrinkage, which will speed up production times compared to more typical paraffin waxes.

Today there are several types of beeswax candles commonly used for personal and religious purposes. The beeswax content ranges from 26% to 100%, though the most common usage is in the range of 51-75%, allowing the incorporation of various additives to raise the softening point and assist with mold release. Beeswax candles are rarely scented, since the wonderfully sweet, honey-like natural fragrance is the primary attraction for this wax. It does blend well with bayberry wax, which has its own unique aroma.

Beeswax comes in many forms. Small block is crude, natural beeswax. Honeycomb sheet comes from a mold. Large block is semi-refined beeswax.

Bayberry wax is very brittle with a characteristic green color and a pleasing natural fragrance.

Bayberry wax is obtained from the berry of the bayberry shrub (Myrica cerifera). The berries of this shrub are coated with a waxy substance, hence the name cerifera or wax bearing. When the berries are boiled in water, the wax coating is removed from the berry, and the wax floats to the surface. The wax has a greenish color and a pleasant, resinous aroma. Its melting point is 109-118 F (43-48 C).

Once used by New Englanders, *bayberry* wax is now rarely found. Its low yields and difficult isolation process have resulted in scarcity of supply and relatively high cost. Bayberry is often found in candles blended with 30-50% beeswax. Blending reduces the cost but also makes the blend less brittle than bayberry and less sticky than beeswax—the best of both worlds?

Petroleum jelly or "petro" has a typical melting range of 100-130 F (38-54 C). It is generally blended with higher melting point paraffins to produce *container fill* (i.e. a wax blend used in container candles).

Candelilla wax is a hard vegetable wax isolated from a shrub (Euphorbia Antisyphillitica) native to the deserts of Northern Mexico. It melts between 155 and 162.5 F (68.5-72.5 C) and has the ability to retain oils. Best known as a plasticizer for chicle (chewing gum), *candelilla* is often used as a precision casting wax with an ability to reproduce exceptional details. It is slightly softer than carnauba wax.

Carnauba wax is the hardest and highest melting vegetable wax, melting between 176 and 187 F (80-86 C). It is a vegetable wax isolated from the leaves of the palm, Copernica cerifera (the palm of life), which only bears wax in regions of northeastern Brazil where climatic conditions offer the perfect balance of rain and heat. Each tree produces about one kilogram (2.2 pounds) of wax during each harvest. *Carnauba* wax is ordinarily used in wax polishes, due to the hardness of the wax. It is known to retain or bind oil.

Montan wax is a mineral wax, usually found in deposits of lignite coal. It is a hard, glossy wax melting between 183 and 194 F (84-90 C). *Montan* is typically used in leather finishing and polishes, though it is sometimes used as a candle additive, especially in overdipping, to increase hardness, gloss, and melting point.

Tallow is not a wax, but a *triglyceride* isolated from the hard fat around the kidneys of cows, sheep, and goats. Tallow was one of the original materials used for candles, but its softness resulted in bending or sagging in the summer heat. Since early refining rarely removed all the *proteinaceous* material associated with the fat, tallow candles also tended to smell when burned and often smoked due to the poor quality of the wicking available to the common man.

Today refined and hardened tallow (and hardened soybean oil) is available for those wanting to reproduce early candlemaking with a slightly modern modification. Triglycerides such as tallow or *hard tallow* are usually blended with paraffin waxes. Today hydrogenated soybean oil is sometimes used in place of tallow. Often, both of these materials are blended with additives to improve hardness and heat resistance, though hydrogenated soy does come in a form that melts as high as 165 F.

Both hydrogenated tallow and soy do offer one potential advantage. Since they are not paraffins, the solubility of most essential and fragrance oils is significantly higher. In fact, *fragrance loadings* of 2-4% have been reported. It is possible to overload the fragrance, lowering the flash point of the melt pool to the extent that it could start burning independent of the wick, so caution is always advised when using fragrance loadings above 2%.

Japan wax with a melting point of 113-131 F (45-55 C) comes from the berry of the Rhus phytosterols bush and is mostly tripalmitin (a triglyceride) and palmitic acid. Where the economics permit, Japan wax has been used in candles (added at up to about 30%) to harden lower melting paraffin blends.

Jojoba wax (from Simmondsia californica or Simmondsia chinensis) is produced by complete hydrogenation of jojoba oil, which is a liquid wax ester. The jojoba plant is native to the Sonora desert ranging from around Riverside, California to Baja California and Guaymas, Sonora Mexico. Jojoba is grown commercially in the Southwestern United States. Hydrogenated, the melting point is about 154 F (68 C). Its use in candles is only limited by cost. Jojoba wax or oil can also be used as a mottling agent.

Rice bran wax (Oryza sativa), mp 167-176 F (75-80 C) is primarily composed of esters of lignoceric acid (~43 wt %), behenic acid (16 wt %), and C22-C36 alcohols (28 wt %).

Ozokerite waxes were originally mined in Poland, Austria, and the former Soviet Union. Today true ozokerite has been replaced by a complex formulation of hydrocarbon waxes, generally melting in the range of 140-200 F (60–93 C).

Ceresine waxes were originally a highly refined version of ozokerite wax. However, today ceresine waxes are also complex formulated hydrocarbon waxes that typically melt at 130-160 F (54-71 C).

Soy waxes (with melting ranges similar to conventional candle waxes) have recently come onto the market. These are blends of hydrogenated soy and other vegetable oils. According to some sources, they burn more cleanly and slowly than conventional waxes. However, there is no documented evidence for this.

Wicks

Wicks come in a variety of thicknesses, weights, and materials.

There are three major types of wicks ordinarily used for candles—flat braided, square braided, and wicks with a core of paper or metal (originally lead, but now mostly zinc). All wicks must be *primed* to remove trapped air and facilitate the initial flow of wax to the flame. For the most part, the composition of the wax used for priming is not important; though it is usually similar to the composition used in the candle body itself.

During the process of making candles, it is important to avoid contacting the wicking with water. Because wicks are mordanted, contact with water will generally lead to sputtering and popping in the finished candle, which is also why one should not extinguish a candle with water.

Flat braided wicks curl naturally to the side, exposing the tip to the oxidizing part of the flame, eliminating most need to trim the wick during burning. There is a "grain" to this type of wick, which leads to a preferred orientation. To enhance delivery of the wax to the flame, the point of the braid (shaped like a "V") should be oriented toward the base of the candle. However, traditional tapers are ordinarily made in pairs from a single strand of wick, which means that half a set has the grain going in one direction and the other half goes in the opposite direction—with no deleterious effects.

The conventions for describing these wicks have been pretty widely accepted and describe the number of plies or strands of fiber in the braid. Tapers up to one inch in diameter (that is, most standard paraffin-based tapers) use 15-ply flat braided wicking. Beeswax tapers may need either 18-ply flat braided wicking or an appropriate square braided wicking, due to the higher melting point of beeswax.

Square braided wicks are more general purpose, suitable for tapers, pillars, or specialty candles. There is no orientation with these wicks, since the grain goes in both directions simultaneously. The size nomenclature for square braided wicks has not yet been standardized, though most manufacturers do follow a convention going (from small to large) from 5/0 to 1/0 and then #1 to #5. To give you an idea of the confusion that size differences cause, I am looking at three different wick makers who recommend, for a 2 1/2" diameter pillar, #2, 1/0, and 2/0 wicks. Confusion will remain until a common protocol is accepted. At the present time, the best way to compare these wicks is to look at the number of strands or plies, plus the weight of the wick per unit of length.

Cored wicks, woven around a central core of paper, cotton, or thin metal wire, are meant for two purposes. Twenty or so years ago, many candle molds were not designed to facilitate wicking, so candle bodies were often poured, a hole for the wick was then drilled, and the wick was manually inserted into the candle and sealed in place using a lower melting wax. The wire core facilitates wick insertion using this process. Today most molds are designed in such a way that the wick is threaded through the mold, and the wax is then poured around the wick.

The most common use of cored wicks today is in container candles, including *gel candles*. Here the wick is usually inserted into a *tab*. The wick core has historically been either a paper or lead. Since there is such great concern for eliminating sources of lead contamination in the environment, most manufacturers are moving to zinc-core wicks and some will also offer tin. (If you are concerned that a metal-core wick might contain lead, peel back the outer part to expose the metal core. Try "writing" with the core like a pencil; if it makes a gray mark, it's probably lead. Zinc will generally not make a mark, since it is significantly harder than lead.)

Metal-core wicks are especially suitable for container candles, because the metal-cored wicks burn hotter than other wicks and thus melt more wax for a given diameter. Unfortunately, once again, there is no uniform system for identifying the size of a cored wick. For comparison purposes, look at the type of core and the length per pound, rather than the numeric identity of the wick. Your supplier will either rely on the wick manufacturer for suggested uses, or (if they have enough experience) they will make their own recommendations. Remember that there are so many possible variations in composition that recommendations are only guidelines. In the end, you still have to burn the candle to see that it performs up to your expectations.

Gel candles require either a metal-core or paper-core wick. Some retailers suggest that paper-core wicks give them better burning properties, generating less smoke. There does not appear to be a unanimous verdict on this, however, since other retailers recommend the metal-core wicks.

There are other wick designs for special applications. Candles that use liquid oil rather than wax generally require a wick similar to that used in oil lamps. This is usually a round, loosely-braided wick that fits into a holder. The best known candles of this type are the goblet candles, where a goblet is partially filled with water, a vegetable or lamp oil layer is then poured, and a floating collar with wick is then placed onto the surface and lit.

A variant of this type of candle is the canning jar candle, where a canning jar is filled with herbs or spices plus lamp oil, and a wick is inserted through a glass collar fitted into a small hole in the top.

For more information on wick selection, see our suggestions in Appendix 2.

Molds

Other than dipped candles, molds of one sort or another are a basic requirement, though there are many forms that molds may take. Molds may come in two or more pieces or in a single-piece construction, wick up or wick down. Most candles are now formed around a wick, but some can still be made where a hole is melted or drilled and the wick is inserted after the body is fashioned. Although almost any paper, high melting point plastic, or foil cylinder can be used (with some care) to make a candle, most commercial candle molds are metal, acrylic or polycarbonate, or rubber.

Metal molds were the first mass-produced candle molds, with pewter molds appearing in the late 1400s. Today molds can be found made of tin, aluminum, pewter, steel, stainless steel, and other metals—both formed from sheet metal (producing a mold with a seam) or cast (and thus seamless).

Since metal conducts heat, these molds are often used in a water bath to control the rate at which the wax solidifies. It is important to strike a balance between the temperature of the wax used and the temperature of the water bath. Warm water is typically used to prevent *shock crystallization* that can lead to fracturing; and cooling slowly usually leads to a smoother, glossier surface.

Aluminum molds come in sizes from small votive to large three-wick types

On the other hand, it is not uncommon to pack a metal mold in ice to force fracturing for interesting surface effects. (In our experience, this should be done after the candle has solidified. When the mold was ice-packed during pouring, the wax pulled away from the mold asymmetrically and resulted in an unusable candle body.) Wax temperatures are usually on the order of 150 F, lower than for acrylic or polycarbonate molds, which are insulating.

When using a water bath for controlled cooling, the mold needs extra care. Making sure that the mold is thoroughly dried after use, and cleaning it to avoid rust formation will keep the mold in working condition. It is almost impossible to remove rust and reestablish a polished surface once a mold has begun to tarnish.

Clear acrylic and polycarbonate molds. These molds give very good results with smooth, glossy candles but care must be taken not to scratch them and to make sure they are absolutely clean. One of the most useful types, shown in the center, has a separable polyurethane base.

One-piece, clear **acrylic molds** come in a variety of sizes and shapes. Since plastic is non-conductive, these molds are not used in water baths. They are quite easy to use, but care must be taken to avoid scratching the surface, since surface blemishes will then be transmitted to the candle. (And these molds can definitely warp if dried in an oven that is too hot; ask us how we know!) These molds are seamless, and the resulting candles need little finishing, though use of an internal or external mold release is recommended (and absolutely essential if the candle contains a large amount of beeswax) to avoid mold damage when the candle is removed.

In acrylic molds, candles are generally cast upside down, with a wick running through a hole in the closed end (which will be the candle top). Acrylic molds are usually limited to simple geometric figures: cylinders, cones, stars, and rectangles. There are also some special, small acrylic molds—designed to attach to the inside of larger molds—that are used with high melting wax to fashion an *appliqué* insert on the side of a larger candle. Continued use of highly fragranced paraffin blends in acrylic molds can result in damage to the mold surface, usually first seen as a smudgy appearance.

Clear **polycarbonate molds** are almost identical to acrylic molds in appearance, shape, and use. But polycarbonate is a harder (and more durable) plastic that better resists scratching and warping.

Polycarbonates are also reportedly more resistant to attack by fragrance oils. Long-term suitability, exposed to high levels of fragrance oils, has not been entirely established. While many acrylic molds are essentially flat (that is the bottom surface of the mold provides the top of the candle), most common polycarbonate molds seem to be domed (again this is the bottom of the mold or top of the candle). In this shape, they commonly have "feet" to provide stability during use. Polycarbonate molds are rapidly replacing acrylic molds in popularity.

Two-piece **plastic molds** are commonly found in most hobby shops. They are fairly inexpensive and available in a wide variety of whimsical shapes. They are not as durable as the rigid molds and the candles they produce need more finishing, since there will be two seam lines which must be removed and polished.

I must point out that it is difficult to firmly anchor the wick in these molds and, as a result, it is easy to have the wick slip out of the holding groove and float free. Remedies are either to drill a hole in the finished candle body for the wick and manually insert it, or to "stick" the wick into the groove in the mold using a bit of mold sealer or similar tacky substance.

Internal or external mold release aids are recommended with these molds and the allowable temperature of wax used in these molds is usually restricted to lower temperatures to avoid distorting the molds. Pouring temperatures as low as 120-140 F are fairly common.

Simple, plastic ornaments and two-part candle molds are readily available at craft stores.

Rubber molds are an extremely functional, fast evolving, late addition to chandlery. These are generally one-piece or slit-resilient molds, made of polyurethane or silicone rubbers, which self-seal around the wick as it exits the mold. Due to their inherent release properties, they are generally suitable for handling 100% beeswax candles without the necessity of an external silicone release treatment.

Not only are they mostly used for novelty shapes, but the polymer base is available in a two-ingredient package, suitable for use in making your own molds. These molds are often available with an auto-fill attachment, essentially a small reservoir that fits snugly onto the base, providing excess wax as the cooling candle shrinks. The auto-fill attachment usually eliminates the need to refill the cavity. Today it is possible to purchase the polymer base and prepare your own candle molds (see chapter 4).

Although large molds often have slit sides to facilitate candle removal, the self-sealing nature of the rubbers tends to minimize the formation of any seam lines in the sides of the candle, so special finishing is rarely needed. If you have never used one of these rubber molds, you will not believe just how easy it can be to make a candle.

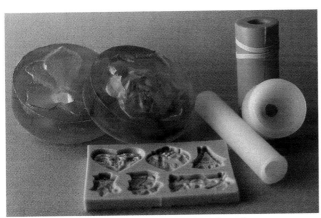

So called rubber molds are actually polyurethane or silicone rubber in composition. These molds are usually used for very complex figurines or fantasy candles.

Plaster of Paris molds can be made and used, though they must be sealed with varnish, shellac, or similar material to prevent wax from penetrating the pores of the mold. Silicone mold release, in addition to the surface varnish, is typically used with this type of mold, often in combination with internal release aids, such as stearin or release wax. In general, plaster molds are more difficult to use than almost any flexible mold.

Sand casting (Chapter 5) uses damp sand to make a regular or freeform mold, which may be incorporated into the finished candle. The finer sands tend to pack more closely and give a smoother candle surface. If a thick shell is desired, then the amount of water in the sand must be strictly limited to the bare minimum, lower melting container waxes should be used, and the pour temperature should be increased to nearly 200 F. It is best to avoid additives that increase the melting point or increase the viscosity of the molten wax. This thicker shell can be smoothed and varnished or carved to form cutouts.

If the newly-poured liquid wax is removed from the shell before it solidifies, it can form a separate shell, which can be carved and refilled with other wax colors. It is also possible to line the sand mold with aluminum foil (sprayed with a silicone release agent), providing a removable barrier for a freeform mold. Surface smoothing of sand-cast candles generally requires the use of a small butane or propane torch, so there are obvious fire hazards to consider. Wire-core wicks, generally tabbed, are inserted into the candle after a thin layer of wax has solidified.

Many manufacturers list the capacity of their molds along with the description of the mold. Unfortunately, this is not universally the case. And so, we have provided a chart (see Appendix I) that estimates how much paraffin is needed for a mold of a certain size and shape. A given mold will contain roughly 10% more beeswax by weight, reflecting the higher density of beeswax. Please note that this is an estimate of mold capacity. When preparing wax to fill the mold, you should always prepare extra wax to compensate for losses and errors in estimating the volume.

Additives

A polyurethane pellet mold is used to make dilutions of special additives in wax to facilitate accurate addition of small amounts of color, scent, and specialty polymer additives.

Additives are, as the name implies, added to candle wax in order to improve various optical and physical properties. *Normal paraffins* (paraffin waxes) are easy to use and have good burning characteristics for candles. However, they also tend to form large crystalline structures that often appear rather blotchy, especially in their normal translucent state. Normal paraffins also have a very limited ability to retain oil, especially fragrance oils. Furthermore, between room temperature and their melting point, paraffins go through a plastic state, which may cause the candles to sag (droop) or block (stick together).

In order to improve hardness, *opacity*, interlayer adhesion, and fragrance retention, and to impart special properties for unique applications, modern candle additives are brought into play. These additives, depending on their chemical type, may be used at levels as low as 0.05% (50 ppm, parts per million) to as high as 30% of the total candle weight.

Stearic acid, actually a mixture of stearic and palmitic acids, derived from palm oil or tallow has been the primary wax modifier since the early 1800s. It is often called stearin, which leads to confusion since stearin is also a term for the crude, solid fat. Stearic acid, melting at 160 F (71 C), performs many functions in candles, including increasing the opacity and whiteness, increasing hardness and burn times, and serving as a mold release aid. Stearic acid will reduce the tendency to sag; but it may either increase or decrease the melting point of the blend, depending on the type of paraffin to which it is added.

Stearic acid is generally added to paraffin at the rate of 2-9 Tbsp. per pound, though it is also not unheard of to use as much as 30% stearic acid. It is added to the melted wax as the wax nears its *pour temperature* and before the addition of fragrance or colors. Low levels (up to 2%) of stearic acid in conjunction with mineral and fragrance oils are reported to increase the tendency of a candle to mottle. Larger amounts (4-5%) are said to suppress mottling.

Some of the unusual or seemingly contradictory claims about the results of stearic acid addition probably result from an unusual property of stearic. It forms a eutectic mixture with paraffin—that is, it forms a mixture that crystallizes together with the wax, in a specific proportion, until one component is depleted. The eutectic mixture has a melting point that is different than that of either the paraffin or the stearic acid. Stearic acid is unique among candle additives in that it can be added to candle wax at fairly high percentages (>5%) without adversely impacting burning or surface uniformity (i.e. without mottling).

Vybar® is another commonly used additive. The primary function of the Vybars is to increase the solubility of oils, especially fragrance oils, in a candle, while decreasing the tendency for surface mottling at the same time. The Vybars do not raise the melting point of a formulation, but will increase overall hardness, burn rate, and gloss. Vybar comes in two versions for candlemaking, Vybar 103 and Vybar 260.

Vybar 103 is used in waxes with a melting point above 135 F, while Vybar 260 is used in waxes melting below 135 F. Vybar 103 melts at 160 F (71 C) while the 260 melts at 130 F (54.5 C). Normal usage is 0.25-2% (the larger amount is roughly 1 Tbsp. per pound of wax) to enhance fragrance retention; but at 4-5%, Vybar can replace 20-30% stearic acid in a wax blend. One word of caution is that although the addition of high amounts of Vybar will allow you to add more fragrance oil, it will not necessarily produce a more fragrant candle. That is, Vybar will strongly associate with fragrance oil even in the melt pool, reducing the volatility of the fragrance material. Tightly bound fragrance will simply burn with the wax instead of producing the desired aroma intensity. In general, the amount of fragrance-binding additives used should be the minimum necessary to avoid mottling.

Microcrystalline waxes (micros), like normal paraffins, are created from petroleum through the refining processes. But, where normal paraffins are produced in the *dewaxing* of petroleum distillates, micros are obtained from the dewaxing of distillation residues. Properties of these waxes range from soft and sticky to hard. They are added to waxes to improve flexibility or workability and to enhance *interlayer adhesion*. They frequently make wax harder without increasing brittleness.

Micros retain oil and prevent migration of the oils to the surface. The various types of micros available melt from about 160-240 F (71.1-115.6 C). Some varieties will also improve gloss and whiteness, though not necessarily opacity. In particular, the two micros we used gave nice, glossy, white candles that were more translucent than opaque. The normal usage levels are 1-5%.

Micros are often used to reduce or eliminate mottling and to improve surface smoothness in container candles. The tacky versions can be used as wax "glues" to adhere hand-shaped components to the surface of a candle. The harder micros can be used for overdipping candles, often giving a mottled finish when used straight or a hard, glossy surface when blended with paraffin. Up to 30% of hard micro wax is commonly used for a hard surface coating.

Unfortunately we have not found any consistency in the names of micro waxes that would allow you to directly compare products between suppliers. As a result, it is best to look at the uses recommended by the particular supplier and look for key words, such as opacity, gloss, hardness, brittleness, etc.

Fischer-Tropsch (sometimes called just F-T) waxes come from a synthetic process, converting synthesis gas (carbon monoxide and hydrogen) to polymeric wax. They are similar in composition to ordinary paraffins, but have much higher molecular weights and thus are higher melting and harder; melting points range from 180-225 F (82.2-107.2 C).

Although F-T waxes are often used as *clear crystals*, they don't necessarily decrease opacity. We have found that F-T waxes tend to make the body pearlescent rather than translucent; and some of the micro waxes were more effective in maintaining translucency. The use of the term clear crystals is usually wishful thinking, since no additive is currently available to make paraffin transparent. The clarity of paraffin is only an artifact of thin external coatings used to seal the surface of a candle.

Use levels of about 1% are typical in wax blends for candle bodies, but levels of up to 20%+ may be used in hard, glossy coatings. In our experience, wax blends with 20% or more F-T wax are quite brittle and glossy. The gloss is great, but the brittleness may make the shell too fragile, at least with rough handling.

These are candles made with gloss additives (1% Gloss Copolymer 400 (round) on the left and 1% Gloss Homopolymer 617 on the right). Both candles also contained 1% stearin. High pour temperatures are at least as effective in producing a glossy surface as the gloss additives we examined and tested.

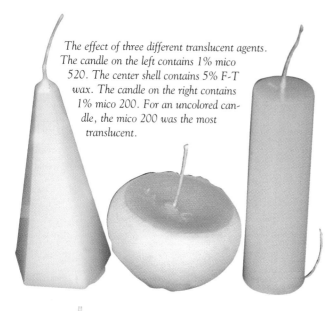

The effect of three different translucent agents. The candle on the left contains 1% mico 520. The center shell contains 5% F-T wax. The candle on the right contains 1% mico 200. For an uncolored candle, the mico 200 was the most translucent.

Candle with mottling oil.

Candle with liquid jojoba wax. Jojoba gives the typical starburst pattern and is at least as efficient as the mineral oils.

Another view of a mottled candle. Mottling oil was added, and the candle was removed from the mold after chilling. Most of the visual defects are horizontal fracture lines, very evenly spaced and located at the bottom of the finished candle. Mottling tends to be more prevalent at the top of the mold, which is usually the bottom of the candle.

Mottling from solid mottling agent. The thumbnail or crescent moon shapes only seem to come from the solid mottling compounds. However, the starburst pattern is more typical even with these materials.

These two candles were made with different mottling agents. As you can see, the candle on the right, made with liquid mottling agent, gives a more pronounced effect than that on the left where an equivalent amount of solid mottling agent was used.

Gloss crystals come in a variety of forms. Some are clear or white polyethylene beads, melting from 190-215 F (87.8-101.7 C). They improve strength and gloss and make colors more vivid. Use rates are typically about 2% or 1 Tbsp. per pound of wax. Other forms of *gloss crystals* are copolymers, such as ethylene vinyl acetate (similar to hot melt glue sticks), and increase release as well as gloss and color vibrancy.

Elvax® additives are a series of ethylene vinyl acetate (EVAc) polymers similar to those used in hot melt glue sticks. Elvax containing 18-28% vinyl acetate (Elvax 300 and especially 400 series resins) has the best compatibility with paraffins, crystallizing at the same temperatures as paraffin wax and forming hybrid or intermingled crystals with improved or strengthened properties. EVAc polymers with less than 18% vinyl acetate can be used with microcrystalline waxes but act only as an inert filler with regular paraffin waxes. Compatible Elvax additives decrease the burn rates of candles and impart toughness, flexibility, and adhesion. Usage levels of 0.5-2% are typically recommended.

Opaque crystals are usually polyethylene (polymer) beads that are used to increase the melting point and opacity of a candle while producing more vivid colors.

Mold Release is not, strictly speaking, an additive since it is a silicone oil or spray that is normally applied to the mold prior to introducing the molten wax. These silicone oils are external release agents, while stearic acid is added to the wax itself and is thus an internal mold release. Silicone sprays may, over time, mar the surface of acrylic molds. If you wish to dip the candle into an acrylic gloss coating, these silicone oils must be buffed from the surface of the candle. In fact, these oils will probably interfere with any sort of dipped coating unless the surface is lightly buffed to remove the silicone.

Release wax is not a true wax, but a waxy fatty acid amide that is added to wax to facilitate release from the mold. As the paraffin solidifies, the *release wax* is squeezed out of the candle matrix and ends up on the surface where the fatty tails form a slippery layer between the wax and the mold. Due to its advantageous melting point (ca. 162 F, 72 C), oleic acid amide is usually the release agent of choice, though stearic amide (228 F, 109 C), erucic amide (167-176 F, 75-80 C) and similar higher melting, related materials could also be used.

Release waxes are also reported to enhance the solubility of fragrance oils within the candle wax base. Some release waxes may, over time, mar the surface of acrylic molds and are often recommended only for use with metal molds. Addition levels of 1-2% are generally used.

Other release agents sometimes incorporated into candles include esters of phthalic acid, especially the dimethyl, diethyl, or methyl ethyl esters. Use levels of these materials range from 0.1-2%, though we suspect that mottling would result from higher levels of usage.

Mottling oil is a mineral oil additive that causes the formation of paraffin crystals. The crystals give a starburst or snowflake look to the candle. Usage levels of about 2% are fairly typical, and release agents are usually not needed in combination with this oil. It has been our observation that jojoba wax will usually give similar effects to mineral oil, and at comparable usage levels.

Other solid *mottling agents* are also available. Though less is known about these materials, they are reportedly solid alcohols. In addition to creating the starburst effect, they are said to enhance fragrance retention in the solid candle body and *fragrance evolution* in the melt pool.

In general, the mottling oil is preferred if you wish to retain translucency in the candle. And, at least at lower usage levels, the oil appears to give very small starbursts while the solid produces larger effects. In our hands, the mottling oils have generated significant mottling at lower addition rates than the solids.

Gel forming polymers are special block copolymers of styrene and butadiene, which (when added to mineral oil) form a clear gel that can be used to make a gel candle. There are many manufacturers of this type of polymer. Kraton®, VaraGEL, and several other polymers are specific brands in use, though they are mostly sold as a pre-made mineral oil gel, ready to melt and cast into a candle. These gels tend to be high melting to the point where it is difficult to handle them in a double boiler, necessitating direct heat to thin them enough to pour easily.

UV stabilizers absorb UV light, preventing color degradation. These are often two-component mixtures to trap both short and long wave radiation, frequently designated UV-A and UV-B. Typical use levels are about 20 ppm or 0.002% (roughly one gram of stabilizer per pound of wax). UV stabilizers are needed for most dye-colored candles that are to be used, stored, or displayed in natural sunlight or fluorescent lighting.

Antioxidants are reactive organic compounds that trap or scavenge *free radicals*, the intermediates of *oxidation*. Many materials, including stearic acid, are not completely color stable and will yellow over time, especially when exposed to heat during repeated burning. Antioxidants are added, usually at roughly 20-50 ppm, to prevent yellowing. BHA and BHT (often found in foods such as baked goods) are the best-known antioxidants used in candles.

Colors

With few exceptions, candle bodies are dyed rather than pigmented. Candle dyes are organic chemicals that will burn along with the wax, while pigments are generally inorganic, rock-like, materials, which do not burn but will flow along with the wax to the wick. As the candle burns, the pigments build deposits on the wick and will eventually clog the wick, preventing the free flow of molten wax to the flame. Candle colors come in various forms: solids and liquids, dilute and concentrated.

For the small scale or occasional chandler, the most convenient form of color is the *dye chip*. Several chips can be added to intensify a color, just as pieces of chips can be used to produce a pale or pastel color. Chips of different colors can also be added to produce another color.

We have to admit that direct addition of a drop or two of a liquid candle color is an incredibly easy way to add color. You can even add drops of color to a molten-wax-filled mold to produce internal color variations. It is, however, hard to use the liquids to make pastel colors, unless you are melting several pounds of wax at one time. And reproducing a particular color is also difficult due to the intensity of the colorant. In other words, you add such a small amount of a liquid color to a pound of wax that it is easy to produce noticeable batch-to-batch color variations using the same number of drops in each batch.

On a practical note, liquid colorants are usually a bit messier to handle than the solid chips. There is usually a practical limit as to the intensity of color you can generate using either color source. With color chips, you are limited to the number of chips you are willing to add to a batch of wax, and since the color is in a wax matrix, you know that you will produce a completely solid candle. With liquid dyes you can generally create more intense colors, but you can be limited by the solubility of the liquid in the candle. That is, you can make a candle that "bleeds" excess liquid colorant. Liquid colorants are usually much more convenient to use when preparing larger, more intensely colored batches of wax.

The large scale or more frequent candle artisan is faced with a quandary. On one hand, we would like to use dye concentrates for economy of scale. On the other hand, trying to weigh milligrams of dye is not feasible for most of us and so reproducibility becomes a real problem and concern.

There are, of course, several possible solutions. One solution is to purchase semi-diluted wax dye chips or blocks that are designed to color 5-pound to 11-pound blocks of wax. The other solution is to make your own semi-dilute colors. In this case, you take the powdered solid or liquid dye concentrate and dissolve it in 1-2 pounds of wax. Casting this in a pellet mold will produce uniformly-colored pellets of a fairly uniform weight, which are as easy to use and control as the commercially purchased varieties. The important thing to remember is that it is just not feasible to use concentrates reproducibly; they must be diluted for color consistency. You cannot even rely on your eyes for color reproducibility or color matching, for there is a marked color change as molten wax solidifies, and the final color is not easy to gauge, even by observing a few drops solidifying on a surface. The color of a candle is unpredictably more color dense than a few drops of wax.

It would be unusual for any candlemaker to keep a stock of every color dye that he or she might want to use in a candle. Most of us are limited to perhaps a dozen colors. However, it is possible to blend colors to produce a complete rainbow of colors and hues. It is important to keep detailed records of your color experiments, so that you can reproduce your color at a later date.

Aside from the conventional candle colors, there are other possibilities for the adventuresome (or those with limited access to suppliers). Many fabric dyes are based on the same sort of chemistry used for producing candle dyes. It is possible to use some (solid) fabric dyes for candles. Water-based, liquid dyes will not mix with your paraffin or wax, and they cannot be used. However, the union dyes, such as RIT, can be dissolved in wax, though it will leave an insoluble residue (basically inorganic salts which are used to control the rate of dying fabrics). Because of this residue, it is necessary to carefully decant the pure wax upper layer from the melting pot into the candle mold. Better still, you would simply transfer the colored wax to another container to be held until you need it.

The only real advantage (other than their wide availability in both grocery and fabric stores) to the use of these union dyes is that color-blending information is readily available from the manufacturer. The thirty or so dyes that are produced (and the dozen or so that are commonly stocked in most stores) can be blended into more than 50 well-documented color blends. And, even if you don't care to wrestle with the handling of the union dyes, you can use the blending charts for a good indication of which candle dyes to blend to produce that mauve or tangerine color that you want for your special candle. The disadvantage of the dyes is their tendency to dye your molds, even polyurethane molds (which are normally impervious to attack). But these dyes are great for use with throwaway molds such as orange juice cans or for use with balloons (see Appendix V, or visit the RIT dye company's Web page: brands.best-foods.com/rit/b.asp).

RIT dye, though not without limitations, can be useful to the beginning candlemaker.

Finished glossy candle. This serves to seal in excess fragrance oil as well as to give a desirable durable glossy appearance.

The very helpful people at Best Foods (parent of the RIT group) suggest that for candles, the lighter colors such as yellow, evening blue, rose pink, and the like give better, more translucent colors than the darker ones. Starting with the basic, packaged dyes, there are directions to expand that color pallet into designer colors. Best Foods also has a color-matching service where they will take a piece of fabric you submit to them and match the color, giving you dye-blending instructions to match the desired color. They are very helpful folks.

There are, unfortunately, a few disadvantages to the use of either dyes or pigments. Pigments, by their crystalline nature, tend to be opaque and so make a candle opaque as well. This renders their use in hurricane or glow-through candles less desirable. Dyes, on the other hand, while not automatically producing opacity, are usually unstable to ultraviolet (UV) radiation. Sunlight and even fluorescent lighting will,

Candle being dipped in gloss coating.

over time, tend to fade the colors of a dyed candle.

Although gloss additives are generally used to produce glossy candles, dipping the finished candle into a gloss coating may enhance gloss. It is possible to use a strippable floor "wax" such as Future®, either dipping the candle or painting the polish onto the candle. Commercial gloss dips, designed for candles, will give a higher gloss level, but floor wax is awfully convenient for a rainy day project with the kids.

Other graduated-color effects can be obtained using a partial-fill method. In this case, a light colored wax is first poured into the mold, but when a reasonable layer of wax has solidified, the remainder is poured out and a second (usually darker) wax is poured into the mold and allowed to completely set. The temperatures of the wax shell and the new molten wax can be controlled to create partial melting and mixing that gives a color effect that fades from one color into the next, rather than a sharp transition line. In the case of a clear wax with a colored wax interior (which is the usual case), the darker interior shows through the outer layer; and if the mold is conical, the shade will vary with the thickness of the candle.

Allowing different colors to mix in the mold is a variation of this technique. For instance, first pouring a yellow wax for about a third of the mold, allowing this layer to solidify, and then adding fresh (and hot) red wax will result in a candle with a yellow top, an orange center section, and a red bottom.

Scents

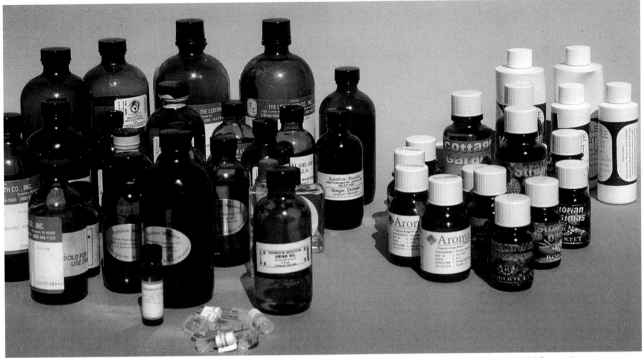

Fragrances, essential oils on the left and synthetic blends on the right, come in a variety of intensities and "flavors."

Fragrant candles are nothing new. For centuries, one of the primary attractions of beeswax candles was the sweet, honey-like fragrance of burning beeswax. Early American colonists soon recognized the aesthetic qualities of bayberry wax in addition to the purely functional properties. Today we use fragrances to celebrate, to establish a mood, and even to help improve our physical and emotional well-being.

The primary method of scenting candles is through the use of candle fragrance oils. These fragrance oils are invariably proprietary blends that may be (a) synthetic aroma chemicals, (b) blends of *essential oils*, (c) essential oils supplemented with aroma chemicals, (d) blends of aromatic chemicals distilled from essential oils, or (e) aromatic chemical solvents extracted from plants.

Since the formulations are proprietary, it is impossible to compare one supplier to another without having the actual samples before you. However, since most candle fragrance oils are designed for a wide variety of candles, typical use levels are usually on the order of 0.75% to 1.5% of the candle weight.

(Container candles often have much higher levels.) The fragrance concentration is important since usage levels above 1.5% may cause the candle surface to become mottled, or cause the oil to ooze out of the finished candle.

Fragrance oil exuding from the surface of a candle. The excess must be wiped off before dipping the candle in an acrylic coating.

It's important to note that these fragrance oils are specifically designed for candles. There are many other fragrance oils, often designed for simmering pots and to enhance potpourri, that are not suitable for candles due to the presence of incompatible solvents or due to the inferior strength of the scent.

In order to avoid surface mottling and to enhance the solubility of fragrance oils in the candle, it is usually advisable to add Vybar. Vybar aids the retention of oils in a candle, either by disrupting the candle's crystal structure or by encapsulating the oil, preventing it from being squeezed out as the wax crystals form.

Aromatherapy, as practiced in the United States, relies on the psychological impact of plant essential oils to promote wellness and well-being. It has long been established that aromas are among the strongest memory triggers. Inhalation of a particular scent may immediately trigger memories of and response to romance, exhilaration, or even terror and trauma. Simply speaking, the theory is that fragrance molecules serve as a key, turning on certain neural pathways in the brain that are capable of doing much more than evoking memories. Optimally, these triggers can relieve depression, increase alertness, calm stress and tension, and even stimulate the body's ability to fight disease (by increasing the activity of the auto-immune system). There is even some debate as to the ability of the essential oils to enter the body through the nasal mucous membranes (via inhalation) or skin (when used in massage therapy) to interact directly on the function of internal organs. In all cases, the active components are the volatile, oil-soluble components of plants and flowers—the essential oils.

It is now important to distinguish between fragrance oils and essential oils.

Fragrance oils may or may not have any therapeutic benefit, depending on the ability of their actual chemical components to interact with the body. Perfume oils, a subset of fragrance oils, are often isolated from plants by extraction.

Although fragrance blending is possible, most candlemakers leave this formulating to fragrance professionals. The major reasons being that chandlers hate to risk losing a large batch of candles on an unproven scent combination, and fragrance professionals can usually do a faster, better, and more cost effective job of blending for a particular aromatic effect. The notable exception to this is in the preparation of aromatherapy candles using essential oils.

Essential oils are chemical mixtures isolated from plants in very specific ways; they have a well-documented history of therapeutic use (especially in Europe and Asia where they are included in approved health care systems). In general, the composition of essential oils is well known. Essential oils are produced only by two methods. Citrus essential oils are produced by cold pressing the rind of the fruit. All other essential oils are produced by steam distillation of specific parts of the plant, such as the flowers, roots, or stalks.

The expense of the essential oil depends mostly on the concentration in the plant material, which relates to the amount of material that must be processed to produce a pound of oil. For some, a few hundred pounds of plant material might make a pound of oil, while others require tons of material to produce a single ounce, and many fragrant plants do not yield an essential oil at all.

The ultimate success in producing aromatherapy candles will depend on the solubility of the essential oil in the wax at concentrations high enough to produce the desired aroma level. As previously stated, this is often easier with container candles, because there is less worry of having the fragrance chemicals migrate to the candle surface. There are some unique tricks, however, to fool the candle into accepting higher than normal levels of oil.

You can pour an unscented outer shell of high melting point wax and use a lower melting point center, highly fragranced. Thus the candle burns down the center, fragrance-rich portion, leaving a protective shell intact. The best results will be obtained when the oil is sufficient to merely mottle the surface. Too much oil can adversely affect the stability between the layers of wax.

Another common technique is to make a chunk candle (see page 78) where the chunks have different fragrances. This is a way to make a candle with a fragrance that changes as it burns. These candles are often called double or triple scented candles, depending on the number of scents used in the chunks. A similar changing fragrance effect can be produced by making a layered candle (see page 78) with different fragrances in each layer.

Since both fragrance and essential oils are water insoluble, there have been attempts to promote candle emission by pre-saturating the wick with fragrance material prior to pouring the candle. While this seems like a good idea, in fact the fragrance of a candle comes almost entirely from fragrance volatilized (evaporated) from the candle's melt pool. The wick leads directly to the flame, and fragrance in the wick is pulled into the combustion zone and destroyed. It can be effective to light a plain, unscented candle and add drops of essential oil to the edge of the melt pool. In this way, the unscented candle can be used to provide a variety of fragrances over its lifetime. It is important to note that the larger the melt pool, the more fragrant the candle can be. For this reason, container candles (with their large melt pool) can be more fragrant than pillar candles.

Best selling essential oils (according to Camden-Grey) include: lavender, peppermint, cinnamon, orange, lemon, litsea cubeba, cedar wood, and patchouli. Aromatherapy practitioners' choices include: lavender, sandalwood, peppermint, eucalyptus, rosemary, tea tree, geranium, rose, various types of citrus (especially bergamot and lemon), clary sage, frankincense, patchouli, and chamomile. Best selling fragrances, according to several of our suppliers, include: lavender, vanilla, rose, mango kiwi, china musk, cantaloupe, jasmine, magnolia, almond, apple spice, lilac, gardenia, apple, chocolate, musk, cucumber, vanilla musk, ocean mist, and pear.

German chamomile, a fern-like annual.

CHAPTER 3
Three Simple Projects for Beginners

How far that little candle throws his beams!
So shines a good deed in a naughty world.

William Shakespeare in *The Merchant of Venice*

Lilac-scented Pillar Candle

My favorite molds are acrylics or polycarbonates, because they are simple to use and you can see what is going on inside. Our first candle will be a lilac-scented pillar candle.

To make this candle, you will need:

* A pillar mold (We used a clean, dry 1" diameter mold.)
* Paraffin wax (We used 135 F melting wax. Canning paraffin from the store is fine.)
* A heat source
* Thermometer
* Pot of water
* Wax melting container
* Wick (We used an 18-ply, flat braided wick, easily obtained from a craft store.)
* Color dye (We used violet.)
* Lilac fragrance oil
* Stearic acid
* Vybar 103 (optional)

Priming the wick

Candle wicks can be primed in the wax for a particular candle, or you can prime a longer piece of wick in paraffin for future use.

The untreated wick is curled up into the molten wax.

The wick is soaked in the paraffin until the air has been replaced with wax. There will be no more bubbles clinging to the wick.

A coil of wick ready to be removed from the paraffin.

Removing the primed wick from the paraffin.

The hot wick should be straightened by gentle pulling.

Procedure:

1. Although you can prime the wick using the same wax that you will use for your candle, we like to use a very small container, so we don't have to fish the wick out of a large can. A small pet-food can works well.

Put enough wax into the small container to roughly half fill it. When the wax is melted, submerge the wick completely in the wax. Leave it for five to ten minutes, swishing it around gently a time or two to facilitate escape of air bubbles while the wax penetrates the wick. Then remove the wick, and gently pull it taut until the wax hardens.

2. Estimate the amount of wax needed for your candle(s) (see Appendix I for mold capacities), and put the wax into the melting container. Put the melting container into a pot of water. The water should cover at least half of the container, so you get good heat transfer. Melt the wax and check the temperature, using a thermometer that reads from roughly 140 F to just over 200 F. While you are heating the wax, prepare (wick) the mold.

3. Thread the primed wick through the hole in the bottom of the mold, and continue pushing it through until you have a few inches above the mold. Tie the excess wick to a skewer or nail, and gently pull the wick at the bottom of the mold until the skewer rests snugly on the rim of the mold. Secure the wick to the bottom of the mold with wick sealer.

Melting wax

The simplest wax melters are clean coffee cans. They are inexpensive and can be dedicated to a single color and then discarded.

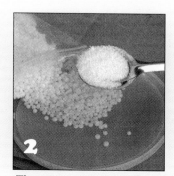

The two most common, and probably most useful, candle additives are stearin and Vybar.

The additives are weighed into the can, along with the paraffin, and melted in a hot water bath.

4. When the molten wax reaches 190 F, add stearic acid and stir until it dissolves. Then add the color chips or liquid dye, and stir until an even color is obtained. Add Vybar (optional), and when that has dissolved completely, add the fragrance and stir again to uniformly disperse the scent.

Pouring the mold

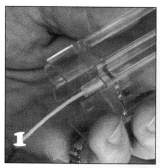

The wick is inserted into the hole in the bottom of the acrylic mold.

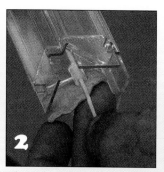

The wick is now pushed or pulled to the top of the mold.

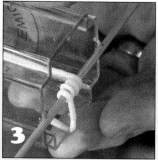

At the top of the mold, the wick is wrapped around a skewer or coffee stirrer.

Mold sealer is wrapped around the wick on the outside, sealing the mold.

Liquid color can be added dropwise until the desired shade is produced.

Candle fragrance oil should be measured into the wax, based on the weight of the wax used.

Taking care not to burn your fingers, the molten wax is poured into the mold.

The mold is filled to the top with hot wax.

Due to the heat of the wax, the wick is softening and starting to unwind.

A piece of mold sealer sticks the end of the wick to the mold, keeping it in place.

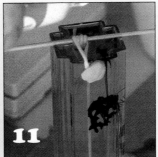

A few drops of blue candle color are dropped into the molten yellow wax.

The cool blue color is heavier than the hot wax and starts to sink in threads to the bottom of the mold.

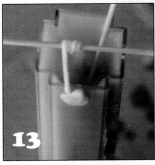

As the wax cools, it shrinks and forms a crater in the center of the mold.

Repouring or refilling the crater.

The candle can be pulled out of the mold using the wick.

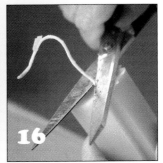

Excess wick is cut from the bottom of the candle.

5. Carefully pour the wax (use a potholder or insulating glove) until the mold is filled to the top. Don't worry if the wax tends to partially cover the knot in the wick.

6. Let the mold stand until the wax has solidified. At this point, you will see a crater in the center of the wax where it has shrunk. If the wax skins over in the center, poke a hole in it to expose the bottom of the wax crater.

7. When the candle has completely solidified, heat the remaining wax back up to 190 F for repouring. Pour the wax into the crater, filling it up to the rim of the mold. You may have to do this as many as three times, until the wax resists shrinkage, and the surface remains relatively flat.

8. When the top of the candle (actually the bottom, since we are making it upside down) remains flat and the crater is completely filled, cool the candle to room temperature, and then place it into the refrigerator for about an hour.

9. At this point, the cold candle should have shrunk away from the sides of the mold. Remove the wick sealer and, holding firmly on to the mold, gently pull the wick by the skewer. The candle should slide out of the mold.

10. Once the candle has warmed back to room temperature, trim the wick and polish the sides of the candle. (A nylon stocking makes a good polishing glove.)

The candle is rubbed gently on the bottom of the hot pan.

The candle is placed on a carpenter's level to determine if you have succeeded in making a straight candle.

11. If the bottom of the candle is slightly uneven, take a small skillet, lined with aluminum foil, and put the skillet on the stove to warm. Then run the bottom of the candle over the warm foil to melt the bottom layer and smooth it off.

12. If desired, coat the candle surface with a gloss finish. Using Future floor polish or candle dip, dip the candle in the gloss or paint the gloss onto the candle.

Simple directions for the absolute novice who has no equipment and no supplies

Wow, that's a tall order, isn't it? Unfortunately you cannot make something out of nothing; at least we can't. But it is possible to start with an absolute minimum of equipment and an absolute minimum of investment—Scout projects immediately come to mind, don't they? That said, we can develop a project that almost anyone can follow, along with a few variations.

Simple Pillars

Equipment and Materials Needed:

* A pan of water that can be heated to, or close to, boiling

* A cat food or tuna fish can (empty and clean) for priming the wick

* A can (empty and clean) capable of holding roughly a pound of wax, bent slightly to make a pouring lip

* Canning wax (available in most grocery stores)

* Wick, flat or square braided (available in most hobby stores, sometimes already primed)

* An orange juice container (empty and clean), with one end removed

* Measuring spoons

* A small piece of modeling clay, Mortite®, or florist clay

* A thin dowel or nail long enough to rest atop the orange juice can

* A drill with a bit just larger than the wicking

* RIT fabric dye

* Can of silicone spray (Check someone's garage; this is often used as a lubricant. If you just cannot get silicone spray, try a heat resistant vegetable oil, such as peanut.)

* Optional, but very desirable: Stearic acid or stearin (available in hobby shops)

A hole is created for the wick by hammering a nail into the top of the can.

Although it is not absolutely necessary, a little silicone lubricant spray will facilitate later separation of the candle from the mold.

The wick is inserted through the hole and completely through the can. It is then sealed on the outside with a piece of wick sealer.

A very simple home setup involves a hot plate, a large can for water, a three-liter metal olive oil can, and a wax thermometer.

Once the wax is melted, color and fragrance are added and mixed into the paraffin.

The wax is carefully poured into the can mold. The can is hot! A towel, gloves, or potholder is very useful to keep from getting burned.

The solidified candle is ready to be removed from the mold.

The cardboard can is simply peeled away from the candle.

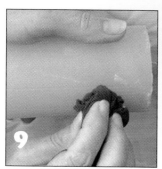

Candles made with this kind of mold should be buffed with an old nylon stocking.

A readily available gloss coating can be applied using an acrylic floor wax.

For a nice finishing touch, a stencil and acrylic paints were used to apply a fleur-de-lis on the candle.

Gluing on flower petals embellishes the candle.

Procedure:

1. Follow the directions on page 33 for priming the wick.

2. Drill or punch a hole in the center of the orange juice can lid.

3. Spray the entire inside of the can with silicone spray, and gently wipe off any excess.

4. Insert the wick, through the bottom hole, until the wick stretches about 2" above the rim of the can.

5. Leaving about 1" of wick protruding through the lid, fix the wick in place using putty or clay.

6. Place the dowel or nail atop the can, in the center, and wrap the wick around the dowel, pulling it taut. You might be able to knot it. Trim off any unneeded wick.

7. Heat the pan of water to simmer, put the paraffin into the larger can, and set this can in the pan of hot water. When the wax is completely melted, wait an additional five minutes.

8. Add 2-4 Tbsp. of stearin, and stir until it is melted and well mixed with the paraffin. This is not essential, but it will raise the melting point of the canning wax and assist in removing the candle from its makeshift mold. It will also make the colors a bit brighter.

9. Add 1-2 teaspoons of RIT dye, and stir well to disperse the dye. The RIT dye should be uniformly dispersed. If you want to make a blended color, mix the dry powders thoroughly, and then use the required amount of the blended powders.

10. Add any (optional) candle scent, if available and desired.

11. Carefully pour the paraffin into the mold and let it congeal (solidify).

12. As the wax cools, it will create a crater in the center. If it skins over, poke a hole in the surface of the crater and pour additional wax. Repeat this step until any crater formed on cooling is minimal.

13. When the candle and mold have completely cooled to room temperature, put them in the refrigerator or freezer for 30-60 minutes. This will also help with removal of the candle from the mold.

14. Remove the putty or clay from the wick. Unwind the wick from the dowel. And, grasping the wick, pull the candle from the mold. If the candle remains stuck, the paper can be pealed off to expose the candle.

15. Gently hand-buff the surface of the candle with an old piece of nylon.

Corrugated Pillars

This project uses corrugated paper sealed with a lacquer or varnish. This will create a corrugated surface to the candle. It requires a few extra steps, but is really quite simple and can give a very attractive and somewhat unusual candle.

Equipment and Materials Needed:

- A pan of water that can be heated to, or close to, boiling
- A cat food or tuna fish can (empty and clean) for priming the wick
- A can (empty and clean) capable of holding roughly a pound of wax, bent slightly to make a pouring lip
- Canning wax (available in most grocery stores)
- Wick, flat or square braided (available in most hobby stores, sometimes already primed)
- A soup can (empty and clean), one end completely removed
- Corrugated paper
- Spray varnish or similar sealer
- Masking or duct tape
- Measuring spoons
- A small piece of modeling clay, Mortite, or florist clay
- A thin dowel, or nail, long enough to rest atop the soup can
- A drill with a bit just larger than the wicking
- RIT fabric dye
- Can of silicone spray (or a heat resistant vegetable oil, such as peanut)
- Optional, but very desirable: Stearic acid or stearin (available in hobby shops)
- Optional: Candle scent, as desired

Corrugated pillars

The tabbed wick is inserted in the bottom of the soup can and held in place with wooden skewers.

Molten wax is poured into the center of the mold and allowed to harden.

Once the candle has been removed from the can, the corrugated paper is gently peeled away from the candle.

Procedure:

1. Follow the directions on page 33 for priming the wick.

2. Drill or punch (with a nail) a hole in the top of the soup can, slightly larger than the wick.

3. Cut the corrugated paper to a size that can be formed into a tube to fit flush inside the can, extending somewhat above the top of the can.

4. Spray the uneven side of the corrugated paper with sealer and allow it to dry. Make sure that the surface is entirely sealed.

5. Form the paper into a tube, and tape the edges together from top to bottom.

6. Spray the inside of the paper tube and the bottom of the can with the silicone spray lubricant. Make sure all surfaces are covered.

7. Thread the wick through the bottom of the can, and pull it through the paper tube until it is several inches above the top.

8. Trim the bottom part of the wick (below the can), leaving about an inch, and seal the hole with Mortite, putty, or mold sealer.

9. Place the dowel across the top of the paper mold, and wrap the wick around the dowel.

10. Following the directions for simple pillars, melt the wax along with the optional stearin, and add color and fragrance as desired.

11. Carefully pour the paraffin into the mold, and let it solidify and cool.

12. As the wax cools, it will create a well or crater in the center. Repour as necessary.

13. Place the cooled mold in the refrigerator for 30-60 minutes.

14. Remove the putty from the wick, and unwind the wick from the dowel. Then, grasping the free end of the wick, pull the paper wrapped candle from the can. If the candle sticks, wax may have seeped outside of the corrugated paper. Use a hair dryer to gently heat the can surface until you can remove the candle.

15. Gently peel off the corrugated paper from the candle. Trim the wick as desired. If needed, the bottom of the candle may be flattened and the ridges may be polished or a gloss coating may be applied.

Dipped Tapers

The materials and ingredients for dipped tapers are essentially the same as for pillars, except you will not need a mold and you will need a dip tank that is taller than the length of the taper you intend to make. A thermometer reading from 100-200°F would really be helpful, because while pillars are usually poured at or near the boiling temperature of the wax, tapers are formed near the congealing point, typically around 140-150°F. It is hard to maintain the correct temperature without a thermometer.

Equipment and Materials Needed:

* A pan of water that can be heated
* A cat food or tuna fish can (empty and clean) for priming the wick
* A can (empty and clean) capable of holding a depth of wax greater than the desired length of the taper
* Canning wax, available in most grocery stores
* Wick, flat or square braided (available in most hobby stores, sometimes already primed)
* Measuring spoons
* RIT fabric dye
* Optional, but very desirable: Stearic acid or stearin (available in hobby shops)
* Optional: Candle scent, as desired (most tapers are unscented)

Dipped tapers

A flat braided wick is placed into a notch cut into a piece of cardboard. This device will be used to facilitate the various cooling stages of dipping.

An ordinary milk carton may be used to rest the tapers between steps.

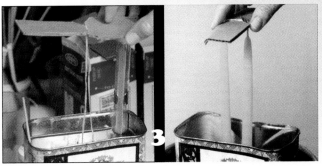

Primed wicks are dipped into the molten wax.

In between wax dips, the tapers are dipped into cool water.

Tapers of virtually any length or thickness may be prepared.

Procedure:

1. Follow the directions on page 33 for priming the wick.

2. Heat the pan of water to simmer. Put the paraffin into the larger can to make the dip tank, and set this can in the pan of hot water. When the wax is completely melted, wait an additional five minutes.

3. Add 2-4 tablespoons of stearin, and stir until it is melted and well mixed with the paraffin. This is not essential, but it will make the colors a bit brighter.

4. Add 1-2 teaspoons of RIT dye (optional) and stir well to disperse the dye.

5. Add any (optional) candle scent, if available and desired.

6. Allow the wax temperature to cool to the point where a skin starts to form on the surface, and then reheat to just above this temperature, roughly 140 F.

7. Hold the primed wick about 1" above the desired length, and dip the wick up to the correct level. Raise the wick completely out of the wax, and let it cool for 20-30 seconds.

8. Continue dipping the wick, allowing the wax to build up around it until the desired thickness has been reached. As the thickness increases, the wax will also extend below the bottom of the wick. This extra wax will be trimmed off later.

9. When the taper has reached the desired dimensions, let it cool for 1-2 minutes, and then straighten it by rolling it gently on a smooth, hard surface.

10. Using a sharp knife, trim the bottom up to the start of the wick.

11. Gently hand-buff the surface of the candle with an old piece of nylon.

Rolled Candles

1. Select a piece of wick about 2" longer than the desired candle length, and prime the wick according to the general directions on page 33.

2. Lay out the beeswax sheet, and cut it on the diagonal, in the long direction.

3. Lay the wick on the long, straight edge, and begin rolling the wax around the wick until you have a nice, tight spiral.

4. Trim the wick.

Beeswax honeycomb

Honeycomb beeswax sheets are readily available at craft stores and can easily be used to make a rolled taper candle.

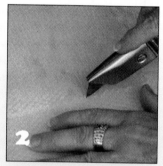

The beeswax sheet is cut into a rectangle.

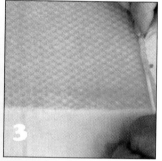

The candle is rolled up around the wick.

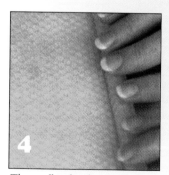

The candle takes form as the rolling continues.

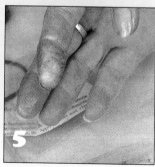

A gold colored powder is being used to change the surface effects on a honeycomb candle.

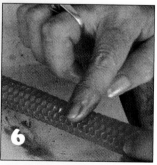

The powder is simply rubbed on the surface of the candle. Additional rubbing or gentle warming with a hair dryer will enable more of the powdered color to be applied.

Multiple colors

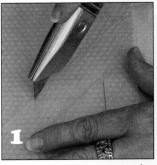

Spiral beeswax tapers start out by cutting a honeycomb sheet into a triangle.

A second contrasting color is cut into a smaller triangle.

The larger triangle is placed atop the smaller one, and the wick is placed along the edge.

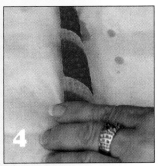

The wax is rolled around the wick along the straight edge.

Making your own wax sheets

The simplest way to make your own wax sheets requires a large vat of molten wax, not something suitable for most new candlemakers. But you can dip a sheet of glass into a wax vat to generate a thin film of wax over the surface of the glass. Repeated dipping will let you build up the thickness to the desired degree. The wax layer can then be carefully pulled off the glass and used to make rolled candles.

For those candlemakers with smaller equipment, take a sheet of glass or non-stick baking sheet and apply adhesive tape to the sides. For thicker sheets of wax, use multiple layers of tape until the tape is as thick as the wax sheet you want. Pour molten wax on the sheet, starting at one end. Rapidly draw a smooth rod, such as a long chopstick, down the sheet to distribute the wax evenly. When the wax has cooled and solidified, peel the wax from the sheet.

CHAPTER 4
Mold Making for Everyone

Acquaintance without patience is like a
candle with no light.

Iranian proverb

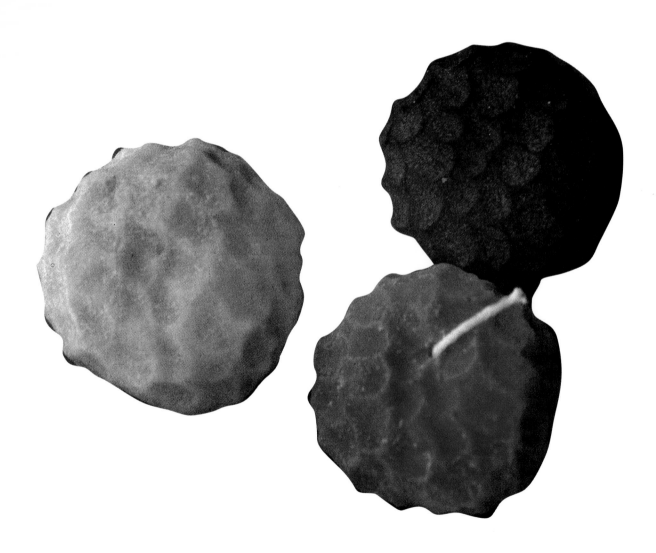

Applying the sealer

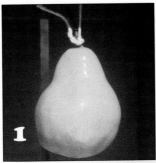

The master object is suspended in the spray booth using the same screw that will be used later to attach the object to the wood retaining sheet.

A spray booth can be made from a cardboard box to aid in sealing a master using an aerosol sealer.

Spraying the sealer in the spray booth.

There are many products on the market for producing molds that can be used with wax to make ornaments or candles. In general, there are two main kinds of materials that are fairly convenient to use: rubber latex and silicone or polyurethane rubbers.

About the simplest material to use is a brush-on, latex rubber, which is applied over a form and then peeled off to make the mold. The steps are as follows:

Seal the object with a shellac or polyurethane coating. This can be either painted or sprayed on. It is best to apply two coats, allowing the initial coat to dry before adding the second coat.

For small objects, mount the object so you can paint all sides and then brush on a coat of latex, completely covering all surfaces. Let dry.

When the first coat is dry, paint on an additional coat of latex and allow the object to dry.

Repeat this step five to ten times, until the dry latex is thick enough to resist tearing. Plan on several days from start to completion of this project.

Peel off the latex from the original object, freeing your mold.

Small molds may be directly filled with wax and, when solidified, the latex is simply peeled off for reuse. The wick is usually placed by drilling a small hole in the wax, after the mold is removed.

For larger objects, it is often most convenient to screw or nail the object onto a small, flat piece of wood. Then the wood and the object can be coated with shellac. When the latex coating is applied, it is then best to coat not only the surface of the model, but also about an inch of the wood surrounding the area where the model is attached. This "lip" can be used later to hold the mold while you are filling it.

Latex mold

A view of the master, latex mold, and finished candle.

In preparation for using a brush-on latex, a pilot hole is drilled in the bottom of the master object; in this case a dried cherimoya.

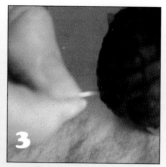

A toothpick is inserted into the pilot hole.

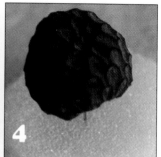

The master object is mounted on a piece of Styrofoam™.

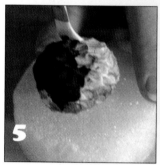

The latex rubber is brushed onto the master object in a very thin coat and allowed to dry and cure very thoroughly. Follow the manufacturer's directions.

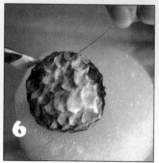

Additional layers must be brushed on to build up the thickness of the latex coating. This took 20 very thin layers.

The base of the latex is slit, and the mold is peeled off of the master.

The empty mold is filled with wax and the candle body is removed by peeling the mold away from the solid wax.

Another type of material, readily available in many craft stores or from good candle equipment suppliers, is a two-part silicone or polyurethane rubber material. This is usually a mixture of a liquid resin or pre-polymer with an activator or hardener. Typically, you mix one part of hardener with two parts (by weight) of the base pre-polymer. The mixture is then poured around a prepared object; the polymer is allowed to stand at room temperature overnight, and then the model is removed from the newly formed rubber by cutting into the mold.

Suppliers often carry several different types of mold polymers. Hard rubbers are generally used for simple, smooth surfaces, such as a taper mold or fruit mold. Softer rubbers are recommended for complex objects, especially if there are cutouts or deep undulations in the surface. The softer rubbers, in this case, make removal of the candle far easier and offer less chance of breaking the candle during *unmolding*.

Select an object to use as the model for the mold. Then find a box or plastic jar that the model fits into. You should have at least an inch of space between the model and the walls of the container and about 1 1/2-2" of space at the bottom. A cardboard box (lined with plastic wrap or a plastic bag) or a suitable plastic jar will work. If you use a jar, remember that you must cut the jar off of the finished mold, so don't select something that is too tough to cut.

Apply at least two coats of shellac to the model, allowing the first coat to dry before applying the second. Attach the model to a shellac-coated, flat piece of wood (usually a screw works best here).

Silicone mold

If the mold is to be filled by volume instead of weight, simply measure the inside of the mold and mark the fill points with pencil using a ruler as a guide.

Mold release is wiped onto the interior surface.

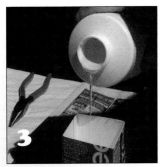

The two components are added to the fill line.

Thoroughly mix the two components using a clean, wooden paint stirrer.

A solid object such as a decorative fruit is prepared by drilling a hole into the bottom.

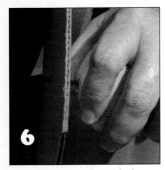

A screw is inserted into the bottom of the object through a wood or cardboard retaining sheet.

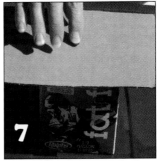

The object is plunged into the casting material and held until the polymer sets.

The raw mold is ready to be slit and the master released.

The paper is peeled away at the end of the cure time.

Apply some silicone mold release to the model and to the inside of the plastic jar, if used. Typically it will not be necessary to try to apply mold release to a plastic bag or wrap, if you are using a lined box.

Prepare enough mold material by mixing the correct amount of the two parts and mixing them together in a disposable container. Once the mold material is thoroughly mixed, pour the material into the container and insert the model until it is surrounded (up to the base) by the mixture. The model will often be buoyant, so place a weight on top of the wood to keep the model in the container with the mixture. Wait 16 hours.

Cut the container away from the solid rubber mold that has formed. Then carefully make two cuts, on opposite sides of the mold, to enable you to remove the model. Don't cut the mold completely in two. Some figures with deep undercuts may require cutting the mold into three sections instead of two.

Once the model is removed, use a needle to thread a wick through the bottom of the mold, wipe the insides of the mold with release, and bind the mold together with rubber bands. You may now pour your wax to make the candle.

If the model selected for the mold is solid (rather than soft plastic or wax), it can probably be reused to make more molds as needed.

In the course of our experimentation to find the best way to make these molds, we discovered a number of things to avoid. Although it seemed like a great idea, wax coated milk cartons did not work well with the polyurethane mold mixture. The polyurethane seems to need a hard surface that is chemically inert. The wax coating produced a very slimy surface and headed straight for our waste bin. A plain box, shaped like that gallon milk container, coated with a couple of coats of shellac would be ideal. A cardboard shipping tube might work quite well, cut to size and coated with shellac. We had very good results using a plastic jar.

It also seemed like a good idea to use a spray polyurethane varnish to seal the model for our mold. After all, polyurethane is hard and almost completely inert. However, this sort of spray varnish did not work with a two-part polyurethane mold material. Apparently the polyurethane varnish really likes the polyurethane mold material, and the result was a mold that was almost impossible to cut away from the model. It may be that polyurethane varnish could be used with the two-part silicone rubber mold material, but that is just a guess. The surest course is to stick with the shellac, despite the mess of dealing with a solvent-based sealer.

CHAPTER 5
Sand, Foil, and Balloon Casting

Thousands of candles can be lighted from a single candle, and the life of the candle will not be shortened.

Indian proverb

OK, so maybe mold making is not your thing. You still have several options to make distinctively formed candles. For instance, you could have someone else make the mold of your dreams. Does that sound crazy? Well, it isn't. Many of the companies that sell molds and mold making supplies will make a custom mold for you.

You also have other options available to you. In the first project of this chapter, we will take a balloon and create a wax shell, then make it into a candle.

Balloon molded candles

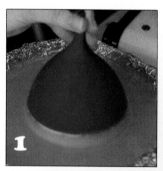

A water-filled balloon is dipped into a pan of molten wax.

Upon removal from the molten wax, the shell forms as the wax solidifies. A complete shell will require twenty or more dips.

In between wax dips, the balloon shell is dipped into cool water in order to hasten the cooling of the shell.

The finished shell is allowed to cool completely.

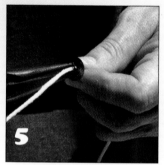

A tabbed wick is prepared by inserting the primed wick through the hole in the tab and crimping the tab with a pair of long-nosed pliers.

To create an opaque shell, take a 145 F wax, add some polyethylene, stearin (to increase the melting point), and dye. Voila! You are ready to make your candle shell.

In this particular case, we are trying to create a more translucent shell, so we start with wax and add 3% F-T crystals to harden the wax.

Take a small balloon and inflate it until it is smooth, but don't put so much air in it that it is near busting—the last thing you want is for the balloon to burst when you dip it into the hot wax. Heat makes the air trapped in the balloon expand.

An alternate process is to fill the balloon with water. The water-filled balloons are a little easier to handle, since the wax hardens faster and it is much easier to dip the balloon into the wax. The water also decreases the buoyancy of the balloon, making it easier to work with than the air-filled balloon.

Heat your wax blend to about 140-160 F. Choose a small balloon, and dip it into the wax until the surface of the wax passes the widest part of the balloon. Quickly remove the balloon, and wait for about thirty seconds (or dip it into cool water to hasten the cooling). Then dip it into the wax again, holding it there for five seconds. Remove the balloon, let it cool for a few seconds, and press the bottom down gently onto a smooth, flat surface to flatten the bottom slightly, so the finished candle will have a flat bottom. Dip the balloon into the wax again, hold it for five seconds, remove it, and flatten the bottom again. Repeat this process until the wax shell is about 1/4-3/8" thick, then let the wax thoroughly cool and deflate the balloon, leaving behind a freestanding shell.

For the center, you will want to use a softer wax, such as a container fill wax, and you will use a tabbed metal-core wick. Start with 125-130 F melting wax with Vybar 260, and add a good dose of fragrance. An easy way to fill this candle is to have the tabbed wick ready at hand and pour a bit of the fill into the candle and then quickly position the wick in the center, with the tab below the top of the new wax. Then, fill the shell, holding the wick upright to prevent it from shifting.

When the candle is completely solid, you can adjust the flatness of the bottom. If necessary, use a foil-covered, hot frying pan (see page 36).

Foil molded candles

1 The sand is partially removed and thoroughly loosened, so that the aluminum foil mold can be more easily shaped in the depression.

2 The foil is placed over the model, and both are placed into the loosened sand and firmly pressed downward to make the mold.

3 The wick is hand held until the top surface of the mold is cool enough to hold it in place.

4 Some decorative mica "sparkles" were sprinkled over the surface of the still-warm wax to provide a decorative touch. Notice that when warm from the wax, they are quite dull.

5 As the wax cools, the sparkles become bright.

6 Both the foil and the wax are lifted gently from the sand. This candle is very fragile.

7 The foil is peeled away from the candle very carefully, so the edges don't break. The foil may be treated with a release agent but in our experience, this has not been necessary.

8 The finished sand-cast, foil candle.

You can easily produce a freeform candle using a base of wet sand, lined with foil. This is the same overall process that we will use for making sand candles, but without embedding any sand in the candle surface. An old washtub or a bucket is especially useful for all sand work.

In this case, start with a wide, flat layer of fine sand. Fill the tub with sand to near the top, and add water until you can make a depression in the sand that remains after the forming object is removed. If the depression fills with water, you have added too much water and need to drain some water, add more sand, or let the excess water evaporate.

A fairly easy way to form the basic temporary mold is to take the forming object and cover it with a sheet of foil. If you want a smooth candle surface, smooth out the foil. For a textured surface, you can crinkle the foil slightly before you apply it to the forming object. When the depression is formed, remove the object but leave the foil in place. Spray the foil with release agent.

Prime and tab your metal-core wick, allowing the wick to remain at least an inch longer than the depth of the free-form candle you want to make.

Next prepare your fill wax. For this project, we can either prepare a hard shell and a softer, lower melting fill wax, or we can simply use a softer pillar wax with a wick sized to leave the outer part of the candle unmelted and unburned.

In the case shown, we simply use a 44-28-18 zinc-core wick with 135 F melting wax. Pour about 1/4" of wax into the bottom of the foil, and when it begins to set, position the wick in the center of the area that will burn. For decorative purposes, you can leave large expanses of wax in remote areas of the mold. Large objects such as shells or other decorative materials can be placed in these areas before the wax is poured.

When the first layer of wax begins to congeal, place the wick, and then add the remainder of the wax to fill the mold. If the fresh wax melts the first layer completely, you may have to brace the wick to keep it upright—or just hold on to it until the congealing lower surface grabs on to the tab and immobilizes the wick.

When the wax has congealed and cooled, lift the candle from the sand and gently peel off the foil. If necessary, the bottom can be flattened, using a hot, foil-lined skillet or pan.

There are a couple of interesting variations possible with this type of candle. First of all, you can form a separate shell. You might want this separate shell in order to use a lower melting, container wax blend for the main part of the candle. You might also want to make a number of outer shells, and then fill the centers with waxes of different colors or fragrances. In this case, you form the foil-lined depression as before, but fill the mold completely with the shell wax.

When the congealing wax has built up a 1/4-3/8" layer of wax, forming the shell, the remaining wax is removed using a metal turkey baster. When cool, remove the shell. Container fill wax may be added, along with the tabbed wick, at any time. Remember that the fill should be added at a lower temperature (140-155 F) to avoid melting the shell, as well as to minimize shrinkage.

Another variation on the foil mold is the use of decorative foils that are not removed. You may use a decorative metal leaf in place of the aluminum foil or gently press the metal leaf into the mold after the foil has been sprayed with release. This is a delicate process due to the fragile or tender nature of metal foils (which relates to their thinness) and takes some practice. In some cases, it will be easier to simply add the foil to the surface after the candle has been made—which is certainly a viable alternative.

Sand molded candles

Plastic buckets are filled with sand and thoroughly moistened, but there is no free water visible.

The mold shape is made by imbedding an object into the sand. If the sand crumbles and fills the mold when you remove the object, the sand is not moist enough.

Sand molds ready for casting.

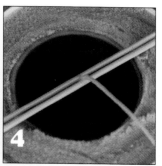

Like any other container candle, the tabbed wick is inserted and immobilized using skewers.

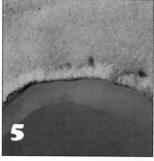

Because of wax shrinkage, it is necessary to pour a second time to refill the mold. In this photo, we used a slightly darker wax for the second pouring to make it easier to see. Ordinarily, this second pour would be done all the way to the edge of the mold.

The candle can be simply lifted out of the sand mold. For small candles, you can occasionally pull on the wick to remove the candle. For larger candles, we recommend that you dig them out gently with your hand.

In this case, the wax was poured at about 180 F and cooled without entrapping any of the wet sand on the outside. When the sand is gently brushed off, the surface is slightly textured and will have a small amount of sand adhering in some places. This textured look is very pleasing.

The basic steps to make sand candles are very similar to the previous examples, but without the foil. In this case, the wax creates a wax/sand shell plus an inner fill all in one step.

Prepare the wet sand as described for the foil-molded candle and create a depression, either freeform or using an object. Prime and tab the metal-core wick, adjusting the length to at least an inch longer than the depth of the candle.

Layered freeform sand mold

You do not need to be intimidated if your sand mold is less than perfect. Who can say just what sort of effect you tried to create? In any event, you do not need to use any object to create the sand mold. All you really have to do is create a depression and fill it. If you pour your wax at temperatures under 210 F, you can even create *layered candles*. One of our favorites was made just this way: Scooping out a hole in the sand, we filled it with layers of pastel waxes.

Remember that the thickness of the shell will depend on the temperature of the wax. The hotter the wax, the more fluid it is, the longer it will remain liquid before congealing, the farther it will penetrate into the sand, and the thicker the shell will be.

A freeform sand mold and excess wax from a variety of different candles can be used to produce a pleasing, layered candle.

Thick sand shell

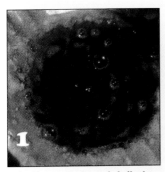

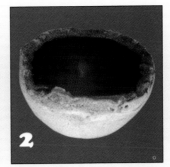

In order to build up a thick sand shell, the wax used must be 230–240 F. This picture shows that the water contained in the sand boils through the molten wax. A lot of noise accompanies such a pour.

When cooled, the sand candle is simply lifted out of the bucket.

In this case, a wick hole is drilled and a wire-core wick is inserted after the wax has completely cooled.

Conversely, the cooler the wax you pour, the thinner the sandy shell will be. If you pour your wax at 140-160 F, you normally produce a candle with almost no sand on the surface. At temperatures around 200 F, you produce a very fine layer of sand. Above about 210 F, you need to switch to direct heat since the boiling point of water is 212 F (100 C). At 270 F, the outer layer or shell of sand and wax reaches roughly 1/2", depending on the moisture in the sand. When you pour at these high temperatures, do not be surprised when the freshly-poured wax appears to boil. It is the water from the sand that is boiling.

When the wax has cooled to room temperature, gently pick the candle up out of the sand and brush off any excess sand. The shell may be trimmed by paring off the excess with a knife or sharp edge. It is also desirable, at this point, to coat the wax (or at least the bottom) with a hard surface coating of varnish or acrylic. This can be brushed or sprayed on, or the candle may be dipped into a suitable material. Ordinarily, this coating should be clear, since colored coatings normally contain pigments that would hide the sandy nature of the surface that you just worked so hard to create. (In other words, don't hide your light under a bushel.)

Since the wax penetrates the sand, forming the shell, it is also possible to make multiple, interconnecting candles by creating two or more depressions in close proximity. In this case, the wax must be poured into all depressions, more or less simultaneously, at temperatures above 230 F. As the wax penetrates the sand, it will flow together making a continuous shell.

CHAPTER 6
Container and Gel Candles

"And then I felt the flame; I felt it burn inside me like a glowing torch to light my way."

From *The Flame*, Flora the Red Menace, lyrics by Fred Ebb

Granulated wax candle

Wax bead candles can be made in decorative patterns by adding the beads to a tilted container.

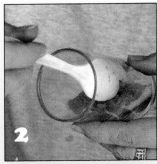

While keeping the container tilted, additional layers are added.

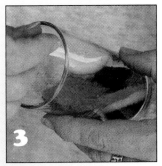

As the container fills, wax crystals are used to fill in the spaces.

A bamboo skewer is used to make "dips" in color.

A wire-core wick (zinc) is pushed to the bottom of the container.

The finished bead candle.

Tin or glass containers are often used to produce a candle that is never removed—a classic container candle. Some votive candles, especially the seven-to-eight-day burning variety, are special examples of container candles. Thermally resistant glass must be used to avoid shattering under the heat of the burning candle. To prevent damage to furniture surfaces, metal containers should either have an insulating base or use a fill that does not completely melt. Mineral oil gels and small wax beads (used with cored wicks) are also available as container fill.

Certainly the easiest type of container candle, and the one eminently suitable as a project for young chandlers, is the use of granulated wax to make container candles. The process is like the sand art frequently seen at craft fairs. Here, as with any container candle, a tabbed metal-core wick should be used and placed in the bottom of the glass container. Layers of colored wax granules are added and manipulated to create a variety of patterns, seen through the side of the glass container. Scented granules are now available, or scent may be added to the granules.

Floating candle

Equipment for making a wax-bead or wax-art candle.

Decorative glass stones are placed in the bottom of the container and then covered with water.

Wax beads are added in a decorative fashion.

Beads of contrasting color are placed to make another layer.

A third layer is formed.

The length of the wick is measured against the depth of the wax by holding it alongside the outside of the container.

The wick is inserted by pushing it to the bottom of the wax beads. Be careful to keep the wick above the water level, so it does not get soaked and therefore ruined.

The candle burns successfully.

Wax beads may also be used to form a floating candle. Although it is possible to simply float the beads on the surface of the water, we have found that water will permeate the beads and lead to a flame that is smaller than usual and flickers more than usual. However, it is possible to take a thin sheet of wax, cut out a shape that covers the surface of the water, and then build your candle on top of this wax cover.

This commercial dragonfly container candle was poured in several layers. However, the different layers never merged into one solid piece, and you can see exactly where the different layers are.

A less-than-perfect commercial container candle. This seven-day votive candle was filled with air voids, which probably resulted from pouring at a temperature that was much too low for the wax. In general, higher wax temperatures result in lower viscosity molten wax and a smoother pour.

A container for a candle can be as simple and as readily obtained as the eggshell shown.

Standard container candle

To start a wax container candle, a tabbed wick is set into place by pouring a small amount of wax into the container. The congealed wax anchors the wick to the bottom.

Pinching the wick between two bamboo skewers fixes it in place.

A blend of paraffin and petroleum jelly is added.

Finished container candles.

Aside from wax art, there are a number of different varieties of container candles, including votive candles, which may be freestanding or formed in the container where they will be used.

All container candles have some things in common. Optimally, they are designed to burn completely, leaving no residue on the walls of the container. This means that the entire surface of the candle should be molten as the candle is burned, forming a large, fairly deep melt pool. Because of this, a low melting wax blend must be used, typically around a 125-129 F melting point. Because of the large melt pool, the wick is usually a metal-core wick that is inserted in a metal tab. The tab and metal core keep the wick upright, eliminating a tendency to topple during use. If the burning wick fell onto the container, it could cause the container to break due to thermal shock. If the wick just fell over into the wax, it would either sink and be extinguished (leaving the candle without a usable wick) or float on the surface (possibly setting the entire surface alight). A hot melt glue gun is frequently used to fix the tab in place, especially for gel candles where you want to avoid adding wax.

Vybar is frequently added to the container blend in order to minimize bubbles and to harden the candle without affecting its melting point. Once the wax blend has been selected, the procedure is quite simple and, except for the use of a tabbed wick, not very different from making a standard pillar candle in a mold.

The secret to container candles is to avoid problems. Typically this means selecting the correct wax and wick size. Container candles are usually poured at temperatures ranging from 140 to 160 F. Although lower temperatures can be used, problems may result. Low wax temperatures mean that the wax has a comparatively high viscosity (thickness) and that can lead to the entrainment of air bubbles. When several layers are poured, there may be insufficient melting between the layers, which will lead to layer separation—not usually a fatal flaw, just an ugly one.

Gel candles

The gel candle compound is a clear, rubbery composition made from mineral oil and a polymer gelling agent.

It is far easier to use the direct heat method, due to the higher melting point of the material. CAUTION! Do not turn your back on gel or wax that it is being directly heated.

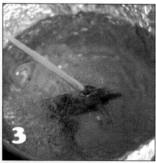

Wax gel in a pan being melted by direct heat. The blue color comes from liquid candle color, which does not detract from the clarity of the finished candle. The aluminum foil lining of the pan enables ease of cleanup.

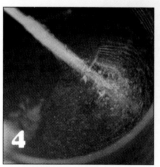

When the gel has melted, additives such as color, fragrance, or pigment (sparkles) may be added.

The wick is held upright by bamboo skewers until the gel has resolidified.

This is a "traveling" candle made in a screw cap jar. It is not clear because sparkles were added to the gel for decorative effect.

Gel candles are extremely easy to make. Unfortunately they are not so easy to make safely. Gel candles are made from mineral oil that has an added synthetic polymer gelling agent. Candle gel is available in low, medium, and high *viscosity* forms.

The high viscosity form is for creating candles with heavy objects "floating" in the candle—marbles or similar pieces of colored glass are quite typical. Low viscosity forms are used to make candles with nothing added except color and fragrance. Medium viscosity gels will support imbedded objects such as pre-formed wax fruit. Glitter can generally be added, in small amounts, to either low or medium viscosity gel.

The difficulty of handling candle gel is the relationship between its pour temperature and its flash point. Even the thin or low viscosity candle gel is hard to handle in a water bath. It is not impossible, but it takes a lot of time and stirring. The addition of fragrance and liquid colorant helps to thin it. Ideally the gel should be heated to around 220 F, which means that you must use a direct heat method, because the gel needs to be hotter than boiling water.

An adjustable-temperature, electric fryer is the best method that we are aware of for handling candle gel. Although you have to be sure that you don't start out heating too strongly, you can maintain heat in the 220-230 F range, and operate with relative safety. It is definitely very hazardous to use any sort of an open flame to handle candle gel. Even using an electric hot plate creates a hazard, since the heating coils are not only likely to be above the flash point, they may well be above the temperature at which the wax vapors spontaneously ignite. However, it is possible to safely handle candle gel if you are willing to take the time or invest in suitable equipment. The lower viscosity gels can be handled in the same double-boiler-type equipment used at home for wax.

Tabbed metal-core wicks are recommended by most suppliers, though a few prefer paper-core wicks. (Most wicks used in gel candles are not primed with wax since the wax may cloud the gel.) One good property of the gels is that they tend to thicken so rapidly that it is relatively easy to place wicks, even without use of a glue gun, and "float" heavy objects during the pouring operation.

Although many are drawn to gel candles by their novelty and the ability to layer different colors or imbed decorative objects, there is still another advantage—scent. In our experience, the scent from a gel candle, at least using lavender essential oil, is much more intense even when unlit than the scent of a freestanding pillar candle with the same essential oil.

There are some extra safety considerations to be observed when creating gel candles. It is possible to add so much *volatile* oil that the flash point is lowered to the point that you end up with a torch (the entire surface ignites) instead of a candle. There are no hard and fast rules as to how much scent is the maximum, it depends on the volatility of the fragrance itself and that (safely) can only be demonstrated by making a candle and burning it. But the fragrance can be powerful, and this is definitely something we would recommend for aromatherapy candles using synergies (blends of essential oils).

CHAPTER 7
Shell Candles and Their Variations

The most common type of shell candle is the hurricane candle, so called since the outer wax shell is supposed to protect the flame from being blown out by wind. There are several types of hurricane candles that can be made, without special molds.

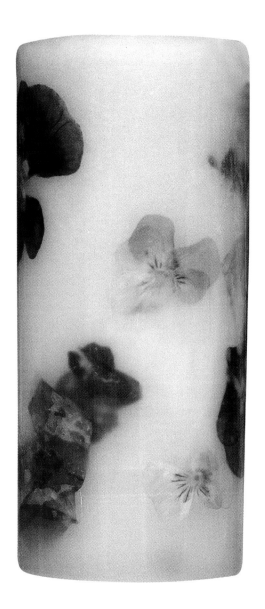

The first kind is simply a pillar candle that is designed in such a way that the flame burns down the center of the candle, leaving a 1/4" or thicker shell unburned. When the candle has completely burned, a votive candle or tea light can be placed in the center. Although it is possible to produce this type of candle by under-sizing the wick (so that the flame is not large enough to completely melt the top of the pillar), it is usually more desirable to produce a hard, high melting outer shell, filling the center with a softer, lower melting wax blend.

In this case, we simply start with a 145 F wax and add a translucent additive (F-T wax) to raise the melting point still higher, without adding to the opacity of the shell. Addition levels of 5-30% are often used, but we have found that levels of F-T wax greater than 20% are difficult to handle in a water bath, since it becomes increasingly more difficult to melt the blend. For this reason, we recommend addition levels of 5-15%. Since this shell is going to last for a long time, it needs to be visually attractive and is normally unscented.

Most hurricane candles are variants on just a few common types. First, a plain, uncolored shell may be painted or partially covered with decals, which can be found in most craft stores. It may be helpful to coat the exterior of the shell with a gloss (or matte) acrylic coating to help the paint adhere permanently to the surface. This shell may be filled with a lower melting container wax blend (and wick) or a separate taper may be placed in the center and burned. Even when the center is filled with container wax, a new taper is used when the fill has been consumed.

It is also possible to decorate the surface with flower petals or similar decorations by painting them onto the surface using molten wax and a paintbrush. Once the surface decoration is attached, you may choose to dip the entire candle in molten wax to deposit a very thin protective wax coating over the entire surface.

A final variant adds one additional step to any hurricane, using a separate (central) taper or tea light. A hole may be cut or carved into the shell, exposing the flame. Although there are special molds available with a special insert that forms a shell around the opening, in most cases it is easier just to carve the hole into the side. In any event, the trick is not so much forming the hole as it is forming the shell itself.

A plain shell may be formed by filling a pillar mold with molten wax (no wick in this case). The wax first solidifies on the surfaces of the mold, forming a shell. When you believe the shell is thick enough, the molten part of the wax is poured out. The only deficiency in this process is that wax rarely solidifies in a uniform coating from top to bottom, but instead leaves a wall with varying thicknesses from top to bottom. For this reason, many prefer to use techniques that give you more control over wall thickness.

One such technique uses an outer mold and a smaller mold for the interior cavity. In this case, the shell bottom is formed over the entire bottom of the large mold using a small amount of wax that is allowed to harden. The inner mold, coated with release aid, is then placed in the center of the larger mold. The space between the molds is filled with decorative material and molten wax is poured to fill the gap between the molds. As the wax cools, the inner mold must be carefully and gradually lifted up, leaving the newly formed shell intact. This technique takes practice, because if the inner mold is left in place until the shell has completely formed, it is very difficult to lift it away from the tight grip of the wax shell. It might be more practical to use a metal mold for the interior, since chilling a metal mold will shrink it somewhat and may facilitate removal.

Hurricanes are conveniently formed in a pillar mold with a separable bottom. Acrylic or polycarbonate molds allow you to view the decorative touches on the surface as you make the candle. The removable bottom greatly assists in removing the shell, since removing the bottom section enables you to push the shell directly.

A small, concentric mold, treated with release agent on the outside, is placed in the center of the mold, and decorative objects are placed around the walls of the outer mold.

The cavity between the inner and outer molds is filled with molten wax.

Flowers are placed around the sides of a mold and the mold is tilted to coat the objects with molten wax. Note that the bottom hole of the mold must be sealed with wick sealer to prevent the wax from running out the bottom during this process.

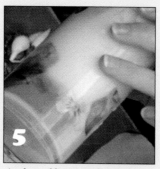

As the mold is rotated to cover all surfaces, molten wax builds up the walls.

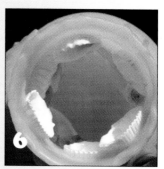

Larger objects such as seashells are imbedded into a thin shell while the wax is still fairly soft.

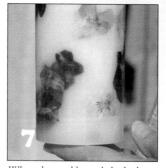

When thoroughly cooled, the hurricane shell slides easily out of the mold. This shell with pansy flowers is a hard, glossy wax with about 10% F-T wax added.

The pansy clad hurricane in use.

In the case of the imbedded shells, the shells are hardly visible from the exterior unless illuminated by a lighted taper inside the shell.

An easier technique to master, in our experience, starts with a single mold. The mold is partially filled with molten wax and the decorative objects are hand-placed around the exterior. The mold is tilted to coat the objects with wax and "glue" them in place.

Once the sides of the mold are covered with wax, the thickness of the walls is built up by continuing the process of adding molten wax and tilting the mold to evenly coat the surfaces. In order to completely coat the upper portion of the mold, the wax is normally poured out as the mold is turned. Then additional wax is added and the process is repeated until the desired thickness is obtained.

It is also possible to imbed objects in such a way that they are only visible (clearly) when the interior candle is lit. In this case, a thin shell is formed as above. Then, while the wax is still soft, objects are imbedded in the walls. Small amounts of additional wax may be dropped or brushed on in order to keep the objects in place. Once the shell has completely cooled around the imbedded objects, add additional wax and continue rotating the mold to further coat the walls and build up the thickness of the shell. If you do not allow the shell to cool completely after imbedding the objects, there is a distinct possibility that the additional hot wax will melt the wax holding the objects to the wall and you will have to begin the imbedding process again.

Almost any (reasonably thin) non-combustible material may be used for imbedding. Millefiore poly-mer clay (readily available at most craft stores) may be cut into slices, baked (to harden), and placed in the walls. Of course, you may also use colored wax slices. In this case the colored wax should be fairly high melting and cold so that the molten wax forming the shell does not melt the insert forming unwanted streaks of color.

Remember that many commercial hurricane candles come, not as a shell, but as a solid candle that leaves a shell behind when burned. If this is the effect you want to create, just treat your newly formed shell as a container to be filled with the container wax of your choosing. Follow the directions in Chapter 6 for container candles or Chapter 5 for balloon candles to make a filled hurricane.

One final reason for creating a separate shell, filled or unfilled, is that this approach allows you to produce a uniformly colored or decorated surface while adding fragrance at an amount that would usually cause either mottling or would risk the fragrance oil actually exuding from the candle surface. The mottling gets confined to the center of the candle, rather than being exposed. The only limitations on the amount of fragrance would be for safety considerations, since you must always ensure that the entire melt pool does not ignite. (To understand this danger better, think of a flaming brandy sauce that burns until the alcohol burns away; or perhaps think of a can of Sterno® surrounded by wax instead of its metal canister.)

CHAPTER 8
Bigger is Better

How far that little candle throws his beams!
So shines a good deed in a naughty world.

William Shakespeare in *The Merchant of Venice*

This chapter deals with the issues involved in making large candles. Tall or wide candles usually create their own unique problems—not to mention tall, wide candles. Most of the issues relating to these rather special candles come down to logistics.

It can be difficult transporting wax from this broad expanse of fuel to the wick. It can be difficult to create enough flame to consume the expanse of molten wax without looking more like a torch than a candle. It can be difficult to produce sufficient molten wax to fill the large mold in a single pouring. Or it can be difficult to find a commercial and affordable mold to make that large candle.

The first two issues are intimately related, since the wider the candle, the more wax must be melted and the larger the wick and the flame must be to melt and burn the wax. The practical limit for a candle with a single wick seems to be somewhere around 5-6" in diameter. At 6" in diameter for a round candle, it is usually more desirable to use three wicks than a single wick. Similarly for oblong molds, candles over 5" in length usually have two to three wicks instead of a single, large wick.

Tall candles

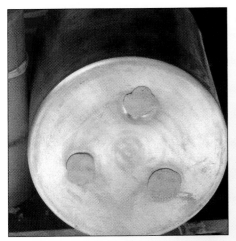

Aluminum mold, 6" in diameter with bottom holes for three wicks. Here the wicks have been inserted and the holes have been sealed with a mold sealer.

Top view of the 6" mold. The three wicks are held in place during pouring by a triangular jig set on top of the mold.

Mold during pouring with a 50/50 blend of paraffin and hard tallow. The wide diameter of this candle and the resulting shrinkage of the wax during cooling required six repourings to fill the craters that formed during cooling.

Finished candle. The tallow/paraffin blend is very brittle, but very glossy.

The overall techniques for making large-diameter candles are similar to the techniques for making candles of smaller diameters. Additives, colors, fragrances, etc. are all considered without regard to diameter. However, where you were increasing the wick size as the candle diameter increased, now you will drop back in wick size and substitute multiple wicks instead.

The selection of large-diameter molds is a bit limited, but they do exist in both metal and rubber. It is possible to pour a large candle body and then drill a hole and insert the wick after the base is formed, but it is easier to cast the candle around the wicks. For a 6" candle, your mold now contains three wick holes and each wick is selected and sized for a 2-3" candle. Although multiple wicks seem tricky, there are devices available to help support three, off-center wicks. In the absence of such a commercial device, one can be constructed out of metal or wood skewers or dowels. In this case, the three skewers are simply formed into an equilateral (the sides are of equal length) triangle and taped, glued, or wired together. Then the wicks, threaded through the bottom holes, are wrapped around the top supports, keeping an eye on the alignment to assure that they rise vertically on a line with the sides of the candle. In the case of an oblong mold, a single skewer may be used around which all the wicks are wrapped.

Since the molds are large, with a relatively large amount of fill wax, the central cavity formed during cooling will be proportionally larger. Two things are especially important: You have prepared enough wax so that there are no obvious color differences between initial and subsequent repours; and the temperature of the wax used to repour must be high enough to melt a substantial amount of the previously poured wax to assure good internal adhesion.

The time required to thoroughly cool the wax in a candle increases dramatically as the diameter increases, since wax itself is an insulator and heat loss is thus inhibited. Another way to look at this is that heat loss, or cooling, is proportional to the surface area of a given amount of wax. Thus the operative factor is the ratio of the surface (where cooling takes place) to the volume (that must be cooled) of a candle. Please note that the units of measurement are not important and the surface-to-volume ratio will be the same no matter if you are measuring the candle in inches or centimeters. The same ratios apply to both round and square candles.

In practical terms, if you compare the surface to volume ratios between two candle molds, you can estimate the relative times for cooling the poured candles. A candle with a surface to volume ratio three times larger than that of another candle will cool three times more rapidly. In other words, if you know how long it took to cool a candle with a S/V ratio of 3.0, then it will take twice as long to cool a candle with a S/V ratio of 1.5, or it will take three times as long to cool a candle with a S/V ratio of 1.

Remember this is just an estimate that relies on a lot of simplified assumptions. In actuality, the loss of heat from the top and bottom of the mold may be greater or less than the loss of heat through the sidewalls of the mold, changing the time required for cooling. However, this table is a good starting point until you generate your own cooling times from your own experience.

There is one final issue that is relative to making candles 6" or greater in diameter. Remember that as wax cools, it shrinks. The shrinkage causes that central crater and also pulls the outer surface away from the surface of the mold, making the candle easier to remove. However, this shrinkage creates stress in the candle body, since the outer surface of the wax becomes solid and resists the forces that are pulling it inward. This stress can cause cracking in the surface. Therefore, the addition of a *plastic additive* is recommended to increase the strength and plasticity of the candle and enable it to withstand these forces.

S/V ratio

Diameter	Height 2.0	4.0	6.0	8.0	10.0	12.0
2.0	3.0	2.5	2.3	2.3	2.2	2.2
4.0	2.0	1.5	1.3	1.3	1.2	1.2
6.0	1.7	1.2	1.0	0.9	0.9	0.8
8.0	1.5	1.0	0.8	0.8	0.7	0.7
10.0	1.4	0.9	0.7	0.7	0.6	0.6

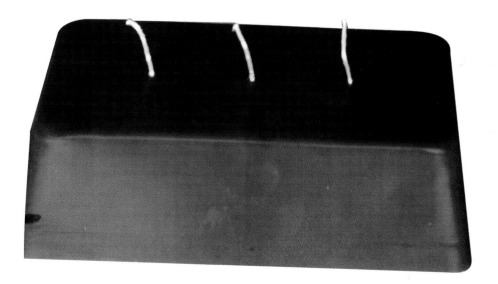

*W*ide candles

Here a non-stick bread loaf pan was used as a mold. The unusual surface appearance, shown here, is typical of wide-surfaced candles due to vibrations as the wax is cooling. This effect can be minimized using a heavy, very stable surface. But remember this surface forms the bottom of the candle.

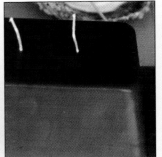

The candle slid nicely out of the pan.

For those not fortunate to have the increasingly expensive large molds, a simple loaf pan from the kitchen will let you make a nice, three-wick candle. Based on the volume of water needed to fill the pan, we estimated that we needed four pounds of wax (figuring roughly a pound of wax for every two cups of *liquid capacity* of the mold).

After only a single repour, the loaf was reasonably full and, after thorough cooling, it slid easily from the pan—much to our relief as we had forgotten to use silicone on the surface of the pan. In this case, we drilled the wick holes after the loaf was formed and poured wax around the wick from the bottom. It would also have been simple to drill three holes in the bottom of the pan and use those holes to place the wicks prior to pouring wax. We did not want to use tabbed wicks since we wanted a very smooth surface to the candle, which meant that the top of the candle had to be at the bottom of the mold.

Candles, especially beeswax candles, are frequently used in religious celebrations. Seven-day votive candles are shown.

Ceremonial candles, such as the Paschal candle shown, are meant to burn during church services over a period of months.

Tall candles are often used for decorative or ceremonial purposes. No matter for which purpose the candles are made, aesthetics normally demand that these candles have no apparent flaws, such as color variations in the wax, seam lines, etc. Since large-scale operations frequently melt master batches of wax upwards of 250 pounds at a time, color variation is rarely a problem in production. For the small-volume candlemaker, however, that is often another story.

Although three to four foot tall molds are rare, they can often be custom ordered from a number of mold manufacturers. It is also possible to make your own (see Chapter 4) using various rubber-type compounds. If you happen to have one of the acrylic or polycarbonate molds with a separable base, you can simply substitute the cylinder of the mold with a longer piece of similar (acrylic or polycarbonate) pipe. Thus a single base may serve to make candles of various heights.

Once you have the mold, the next step is to calculate the amount of wax needed. In general, use the Mold Capacity Tables in Appendix I. If your candle is taller than listed in the tables, just choose an easy multiple. (If you are making a four-foot candle, it will require four times the amount of wax as a one-foot candle of equal diameter.)

With a lot of luck, you may have a vessel that will contain enough wax to fill the mold, including repouring. If not, you will have to meet the challenges of pouring a candle in stages. Although that does not, at first, appear to be a problem, it is difficult to pour a tall candle in stages, leaving no obvious evidence that the candle was made in layers. And that is true even if the candle is not colored, so that color-matching issues are eliminated.

The best approach to filling a tall candle is really to pour it all at once. If you do not have a large wax reservoir, try using two smaller ones. It requires a bit of juggling, but it is possible to get two pots full of wax and get them both melted. It is better to have the two containers at slightly different temperatures (one cooler than the other) than to add new wax to a substantially solid partial fill.

Tall candles, in general, should be slowly poured at as high a temperature as you can manage (compatible with the mold you are using). The taller the candle, the more likely you will get air entrainment (bubbles) during pouring, so you need to keep the temperature high to minimize viscosity; and you should incorporate Vybar or a similar additive to reduce the tendency for air entrainment.

If you are making tall, evenly-colored candles, it is most important that you use less concentrated colors and carefully add the color by weight. This may require diluting your color concentrates more than you typically use, but the extra step will be worthwhile.

Finally, if you are making irregular candles, such as those resembling bamboo or some in-and-out geometric design, try to get your transition from one wax container to the next to occur at one of the irregular parts of the surface: The joint of a bamboo, or the narrowest point of the irregular design.

Of course, you can also make the most of the color gradation problem by intentionally using different colored waxes, designing in a transition form (usually) pale to darker colors with zones where the color is allowed to mix and blend.

CHAPTER 9
Candles and More Candles

It is just not possible for one book of reasonable size to contain working examples of all the fun and interesting candles and variations that are possible. We know, because at times it seemed to us that we were trying to make them all. But though we cannot make and describe every type of candle, we would be remiss without including several additional, interesting candles that demonstrate a variety of techniques. The following pages contain a number of candles of which we are particularly fond, and which we believe are well within the capabilities of chandlers with moderate experience.

Ice candle

Start out with a central taper in the mold.

Ice cubes are packed around the taper in the mold.

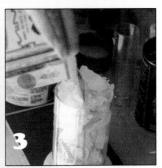

Hot wax is poured over the ice into the mold.

The mold is filled with wax, up to the exposed wick in the taper.

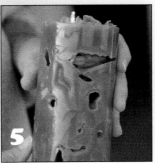

When thoroughly cooled, the water is poured off and the candle is removed from the mold.

Ice candles start out with a preformed taper placed in the center of a pillar mold. It is not necessary to use a full-sized taper. The starting candle mainly serves to isolate the wick from the water formed by the melting ice, so that the candle can actually be burned. Typically, the central taper is of the same color as the candle to be formed; but in this case a white taper was used to make the technique obvious.

This particular mold has a separable bottom, which makes removal of the finished candle quite easy. Since the bottom is synthetic rubber, it is self-sealing and thus has no hole that requires plugging.

Building the candle involves placing the central taper, surrounding it with ice, and then filling the mold with wax heated to 180 F. As a cautionary note, don't heat the wax above 210 F, since the melting ice might actually boil over and cause the hot wax to erupt from the mold.

When the candle is un-molded, water will pour out from the interior of the candle. The lacy, cutout appearance will vary depending on the size and number of the ice cubes used. These candles are very fragile but can sometimes be reused because the taper will tend to burn and leave the lacy shell behind.

Chunk candle

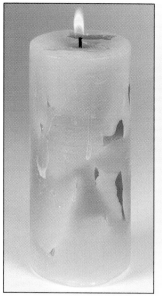

Chunk candles were once strictly the domain of the hobbyist, but now they are routinely found in both craft shops and decorator boutiques. Ordinarily, the exterior of this candle is uncolored paraffin, occasionally with translucent crystals added. Neither Vybar nor stearin are used, since both additives increase opacity.

The first step is preparation of the chunks. 145 F paraffin is colored (using candle dyes, not pigments) and cast into thick (1/2" or thicker) sheets. The chunks may be cut freeform or with a cookie cutter for regular shapes. We recommend that the chunks be hardened by the addition of 2% Vybar or 3-4% stearin to resist melting when the final candle is poured. The chunks should be chilled (covered to avoid the condensation of moisture on the surfaces) in the refrigerator for at least thirty minutes before use.

A pillar mold is wicked as usual, and then the colored chunks are placed (stacked) around the sides. The molten wax is poured at temperatures of 145-150 F; and the finished candle is un-molded as usual for pillar candles.

Chunks that touch the surface of the mold appear as dark splotches of color.

Harlequin candle

The harlequin candle is made in a 3" metal pillar mold using many different colors of wax. The wax was poured at about 145 F, so that there would be only a minimal disruption of color between layers. Higher temperatures of 180 F would result in a much smoother surface, but would produce color blending and distortion between the layers. Although you can use silicone mold release to facilitate removal from the mold, the release will make it difficult or impossible to apply an acrylic gloss coating.

In order to make the tilted layers for the harlequin candle, the mold was propped at an angle and turned between layers.

Color blended candle

A different effect is obtained if the wax colors are not thoroughly cooled and solidified between layers. Here a mold is partially filled with a red wax.

The initial layer is allowed to cool until the outer surfaces solidify.

Next, a blue wax is added, which mixed with still molten wax from the first layer.

The hot wax partially melts the upper surfaces that had previously solidified.

Again, the new layer of wax is allowed to partially solidify before adding yet a third, darker color.

With the third layer added, the entire candle is allowed to solidify and cool completely.

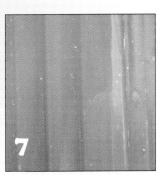

Detail showing color transition and blending.

Floating candles

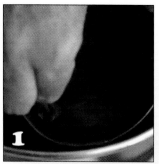

A tabbed wick is dipped into molten wax so that it can be attached to the bottom of the shallow mold.

Shallow craft molds can be used to create floating candles. It does not take a specific "floater" candle mold to make one. The only requirement is that the candle be wider than it is deep. Here the wick tab is centered into the mold and sticks because of the wax.

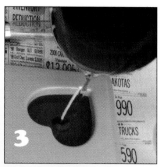

Wax is carefully poured to fill the mold.

The candles, when thoroughly cooled, usually pop out of the mold quite easily.

Finished floating candles.

Wick tabs are visible through the bottom of the candles.

A candle floating in a shallow bowl, surrounded by small flowers.

A deeper container holds full, fresh flowers and a floating candle on top.

A top view, showing the floating candle ready to be lighted.

Chessman

Wax melting for use with a two-part mold. Lower pour temperatures around 145 F are typically used with these molds. The wax (135 F) was colored ivory, and the fragrance was French vanilla.

This mold snaps together and then fits into a base that supposedly supports and holds it together while preventing wax from leaking. In our experience, the snap-together part should be reinforced with clamps or clothespins. Although the mold has a channel that is supposed to keep the wick immobilized, in our experience it is very, very easy to displace the wick once the hot wax fills the mold. We have found that it is often easier to fill the mold without a wick and then drill the wick hole later. It just takes a long drill bit.

The Chessman candle resting in half the mold.

The wax flashing is trimmed using a sharp knife.

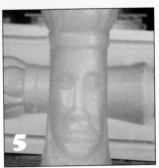

After polishing, the candle is finished.

Molded bayberry tapers

Dipping or using a taper mold may make bayberry candles. These molded candles used 85% bayberry plus 15% beeswax.

Molded bayberry candles add character in a traditional holiday display setting.

CHAPTER 10
Tallow, Bayberry, Beeswax, and Festival Candles

Yes, you can indeed make tallow candles. We have to ask, right away, why on earth you would want to; but you most certainly can do it. There are real problems with making tallow candles.

The major problems with using tallow are the same problems that made tallow less desirable than other alternatives prior to the 1900s. Tallow sags in the heat of a summer's day. Tallow candles can go rancid and really start to smell, even if the tallow is "professionally" rendered to remove protein and other animal bits that would inherently cause a stench.

Certainly all these problems can be dealt with by using antioxidants and preservatives and by adding stearin or modern additives that toughen the candle. For the traditionalists, who wish to make candles the old fashioned way, being faithful to the heritage of chandlery (or for those who want to provide a realistic reenactment for Renaissance fairs and the like), there are alternatives that don't bend the rules to the breaking point.

You can use bayberry, beeswax, or bayberry/beeswax blends, which were all available to the original settlers of the 13 colonies. All these materials can be used to dip tapers as they were made 200 years ago. (Remember that until the advent of modern molds, beeswax could not be used in molded candles.) And bayberry, though expensive, can be used alone (or with a little added stearin) to produce molded candles, using tin or similar metal molds.

But, yes, you can make tallow candles, though we would highly recommend using hydrogenated tallow for this purpose. Hydrogenation reduces the amount of unsaturation, which is primarily responsible for rancidity (air oxidation, rather like rusting, breaks these fatty acids down into short volatile acids that smell). Hydrogenated tallow is much cleaner and much more stable. Hydrogenation also raises the melting point of tallow, so that the hydrogenated version is much more resistant to sagging; and it cleans up the tallow, so it is much less likely to smell for any reason.

For those who wish merely to produce a natural candle, or at least a candle made using renewable resources, you may use either hydrogenated tallow or hydrogenated soybean oil in combination with stearin to improve the melting point and reduce the tendency to sag. In order to further stabilize the raw materials against oxidation and rancidity, without resorting to "synthetic" antioxidants, you may use the oil soluble ROE, rosemary oil extract, which is a fine antioxidant.

This is a special setting featuring molded bayberry tapers in custom made art deco candle holders, resting on a holiday quilt handmade by the author.

CHAPTER 11
Ornaments, Keepsakes, and Other Combustible Treasures

When we think of wax ornaments, we frequently think of Christmas tree ornaments. But ornaments encompass any number of decorative or sentimental objects, including whimsical or *fantasy candles*.

The production of **hanging ornaments** has traditionally used 100% beeswax. Traditional colors are either the yellow of semi-refined beeswax or a Yule red (or more rarely green). Since ornaments are not designed to burn, pigments may be used in this application.

The use of beeswax requires either the use of release spray (silicone fluids) or molds made of silicone or polyurethane rubbers. Beeswax was traditionally used because of its high melting point, which resists sagging in hot rooms. Of course, constructs other than 100% beeswax can be used. Frequently, blends with 51% beeswax (or even less) are referred to as beeswax.

Suggested wax blends include: 100% beeswax; 75% beeswax/25% 145 F paraffin wax; 51% beeswax/49% 145 F (or higher) paraffin wax; 75% 145 F paraffin wax/25% 155 F paraffin wax; and 90% 145 F paraffin wax/10% F-T wax.

Various plastic additives should be used to increase the melting point, minimize sag, and increase the hardness of the ornament. Although the special molds are highly recommended for use with all beeswax blends, the addition of release wax to the blend may permit the use of metal molds. The use of plastic molds is not recommended in this case, since any difficulty in removing the wax ornament from the mold will most likely result in damaging the mold.

Hanging ornaments

A polyurethane mold and decorative ribbons which will be the hangers for the ornaments.

It is usually good practice to add a small amount of silicone mold release to the mold, especially before its initial use.

The loose ends of a ribbon loop are held in place as the beeswax is poured into the mold.

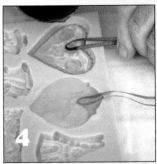

Ornament molds typically come with many designs in the same mold sheet.

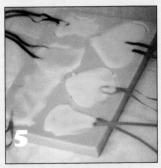

The beeswax is allowed to thoroughly cool before removal.

Gentle flexing of the mold will usually cause the ornament to pop out.

Any residual wax on the edges of the ornaments is snapped or trimmed off.

Finished Santa Claus ornament.

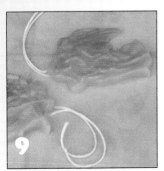

Ornaments, such as the two angels pictured here, may also be finished by rubbing with any of the powdered glitters.

An Easter bunny leaning on his cane shows the sort of cutout figures that are possible using these silicone or polyurethane rubber molds. "Cutout" refers to the empty space between the figure and the cane.

*F*antasy candles

1

A synthetic rubber mold has been prepared to receive the wax. The wick has been inserted through the bottom and is wrapped around a skewer at the top of the mold.

2

The cooled candle is freed from the mold by pulling apart the two halves, so that gently moving and pulling can free the top of the candle.

3

This is the finished Celtic cross beeswax candle, after the wick has been trimmed.

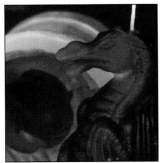

Sculpted figurines, such as the dragon shown alongside its rubber mold, are frequently called fantasy candles.

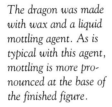

The dragon was made with wax and a liquid mottling agent. As is typical with this agent, mottling is more pronounced at the base of the finished figure.

Fantasy candles are actually wax figurines that may or may not have a wick. They are mostly for decorative uses and are rarely burned. Fantasy candles made from beeswax are generally uncoated or unglazed, so the natural scent of beeswax is obvious to the nose of the beholder. Paraffin wax based figurines, that are not designed to burn, are usually heavily coated with a high-gloss acrylic coating and are often intensely colored, using pigments rather than dyes.

Silicone or polyurethane rubber molds are generally used, since the figurines usually have intricate surfaces including cutouts and extreme details. The Celtic cross, shown in the accompanying illustrations, is covered with figures on both sides. The tough, but flexible, rubber of the mold allows the reproduction of the detail and enables the horizontal surfaces of the cross to be formed and released intact from the mold. We typically used either 100% beeswax or a 75/25 blend of beeswax and 145 F paraffin in candles from this mold.

Fantasy molds are readily available from full service dealers in a range of figures for almost every season or fancy. All the decorating techniques described in other chapters, including mottling, glazing, and highlighting with metallic powders, may be used. After all, they are designed to appeal to your own fantasies.

Fire starters

A primed wick is inserted deeply into a pinecone. A skewer is used to push the wick past the petals.

The finished fire starters have been covered with wax by both dipping and pouring techniques.

Fire starters, though not quite in the same category as the other treasures, are certainly another good project for candlemakers. Most commercial types are mixtures of sawdust and paraffin that are cast into logs. However, you have to be in just the right area or region to have access to reliable supplies of (inexpensive) sawdust. Thus it is often more practical to use something like pinecones as a base. You can use a plain paraffin-dipped pinecone, with or without a wick, or you can add various salts to the wax to produce a product that will burn with a colored flame.

These molded candles used 85% 135 F paraffin plus 15% petroleum jelly, since the object is to ignite the entire pinecone rather than to burn it like a taper.

The type of salt that is added to the wax controls the color of the flame (see table 1). To some degree, especially since you use a minimal quantity, the salts may be mixed. But it is usually not desirable to add sodium salts (such as common table salt, sodium chloride) along with other types, since sodium produces such an intense yellow flame it will mask most other colors. The most commonly used salts are the chlorides, carbonates, and sometimes sulfates. Salts for colors may come from a variety of sources, including candle ingredient suppliers and chemical supply houses.

Table 1, Color From Salts

Color	Salt used
Yellow	sodium chloride or sulfate
Orange	calcium chloride
Red	strontium chloride or hydroxide
Green	barium chloride
Blue	copper chloride

Another type of treasure, **wax hands**, has grown increasingly popular at Renaissance fairs. Although it is possible to reproduce this at home, at fairs the booths have temperature-controlled water baths for the wax. This is essential, since the potential for burns is quite high without very good temperature control.

Reflecting the situation where a naked hand will be plunged into the wax, a LOW melting wax blend is used, typically on the order of 125 F. The working temperature must be carefully controlled to under 140 F, and the lower the better.

In this case, a deep container of the low melting wax is prepared (melted) and the temperature stabilized. The hand, fingers outstretched, is dipped into a pail of cool water, and the excess is lightly shaken off.

The hand is then dipped into the wax, up to just over the wrist, for ten seconds and then removed and dipped into the water. After waiting at least thirty seconds, the wax-covered hand is again dipped for ten seconds into the wax and then again in the water. Typically the hand is dipped about ten times or until the desired thickness is reached.

At this point, the underside of the wax is carefully slit with a pair of scissors until the wax can be carefully slid from the hand. A hair dryer may be used to warm the wax slightly to increase its flexibility during the removal process. Typically, the wax slit is closed again, so the hand may be set upright, or a small dowel, tipped with sticky micro wax, may be inserted into a finger.

CHAPTER 12
The Meaning and Symbolism of Color

What color is the wind?
Dolly–*The Family Circus* by Bil Keane

A color "wheel" blanket woven by the author shows not only pure colors but also how they blend and change when they interact with one another.

Color is a deceptively simple subject with many aspects and nuances. On the surface, color is described by only three factors—hue, value, and chroma or intensity. However, color and color combinations also have emotional and social appeal, and so aspects of temperature and psychological impact are also important. All these factors need to be considered for decorating with color, for blending basic wax colors to create new colors, or to create interesting and attractive visual effects by the combination of colors within a single object.

The first dimension of color is hue, which is the family name of a specific color such as red. Within the red color family (hue) are bright vivid reds such as scarlet, and dull or darker reds such as burgundy. Within any color family are tints (lighter colors formed by adding white) and shades (darker colors formed by adding black).

Higher or lighter values reflect more light than lower (darker) values. Picture a light blue sky above a dark blue sea; the image has the same hue but widely differ-ent values. Value is considered the most important aspect of color, partly because value differences often create three-dimensional visual effects (or at least allow us to see in three-dimensions).

Chroma (intensity) is the aspect of color that refers to the perceived brightness (or saturation) of color. Think of a glossy intense black next to a dull, matte black. The former color has a higher chroma. A color with a high degree of chroma is pure or not grayed by the addition of any other color. A color that is closer to an earth tone or is closer to neutral is of low chroma. The chroma of a color is most frequently reduced by the addition of a complementary color.

The three colors, which are the beginning, or the source, of all other colors are called primary colors—red, yellow, and blue. Mixing two or more primary colors produces all other colors. Secondary colors are achieved by mixing two primary colors in equal proportions (that is a 1:1 ratio). Red plus yellow is orange. Red plus blue is violet. Yellow plus blue is green. The secondary colors are orange, violet, and green.

Two secondary colors mixed in equal proportions will give a tertiary color. All three primary colors are included in the final result. Orange plus green results in olive. Orange and violet make rust. Violet plus green makes navy blue. The tertiary colors are not as bright as the primary and secondary colors.

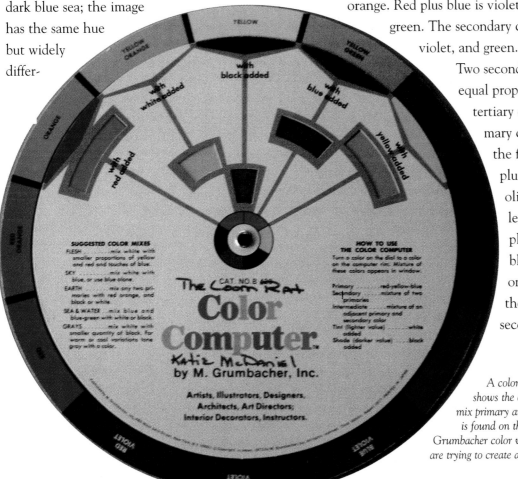

A color computer is a device that shows the colors that result when you mix primary and/or secondary colors. This is found on the back of the traditional Grumbacher color wheel. It is useful when you are trying to create a color to match another.

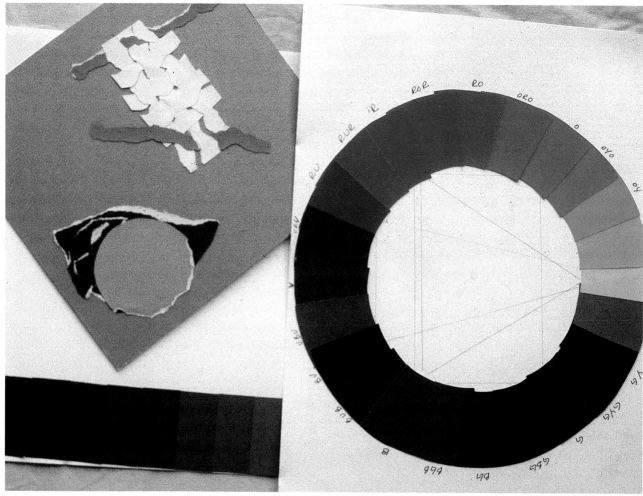

A handmade gray scale and color harmony wheel can help select and coordinate color schemes.

The color wheel is the most useful visual tool for understanding color usage. The hub of the wheel is comprised of the primary colors along with the secondary colors, prepared by mixing equal parts of each pair of primary colors. The outer section of the wheel contains a progression of primary and secondary colors along with the mixtures of primary with secondary, e.g. red, red-orange, orange, etc.

Color harmony plays a major role in design. Monochromatic harmony is harmony of only one color or hue but varying in shade and tone. Analogous harmony includes the three to five colors that are next to one another on the color wheel. They resemble one another. One example of analogous color is red, red orange, orange, and yellow orange.

Those colors that lie directly opposite one another on the color wheel are called complementary. Red is the complement to green; Violet is the complement to yellow; and blue is the complement to orange.

Proportion enters the discussion of color simply because proportion can alter the perception of color. Stripes of red and green of equal width will not appear to be of the same width. The red will seem a bit wider. Yellow will advance from blue and appear to be closer to the observer. Blue will appear to have more spatial depth when next to yellow. Blue next to yellow will appear to have a harder edge. In very fine detail, proportion becomes very important.

Temperature refers to a color's perceived warmth or coolness. Blue, for example, will usually be perceived as cold and orange as hot. Colors such as violet contain both a warm (red) and a cool (blue) element and express a temperature relative to their neighbors. Around the color wheel, warm colors are grouped to one side and cool colors to the other. Still, contrasts of temperature—important considerations in any color selection process—usually relate to a specific design and provide yet another important aspect for exploring the expressive possibilities of color.

The color wheel helps us understand these aspects of color. A line bisecting the wheel, drawn through yellow-green to red-violet, divides the wheel into cool colors and warm colors. The two colors bisected by the line as well as transition colors can be considered to fit into both or neither category.

Warm colors are invigorating and exciting. They intensify heat and are often used to warm a cool room with a northern exposure. Warm colors are great for studios and work areas or sickrooms. Cool colors are relaxing and calm, often used in bedrooms and

where the sun might become unbearably bright and hot.

Complementary colors blend well in two ways. First, they can be used together in arrangements. Second, they mix well. A common way to darken a color is to blend in a small amount of its complementary color. Color wheels, which are designed to predict blended colors or to help produce desired colors by blending, are often called color calculators and are extremely useful tools to assist in producing specific colors of candles.

Color plays a psychological and symbolic role. It is an important facet in our culture, religions, and daily lives no matter which culture we spring from. That is not to say that the implications or symbolism of color are constant. In Western culture, white is a symbol of purity and innocence; in Eastern culture, it is the color of death and mourning. Today, in Western culture, white is the color for weddings; but centuries ago green (with its implications of fertility and fortune) was considered a much more common and appropriate color. But with this very brief discussion serving as a warning that not all cultures will view color symbolism in the same "light," the following is a summary of common (mostly Western) symbolism of colors and candles.

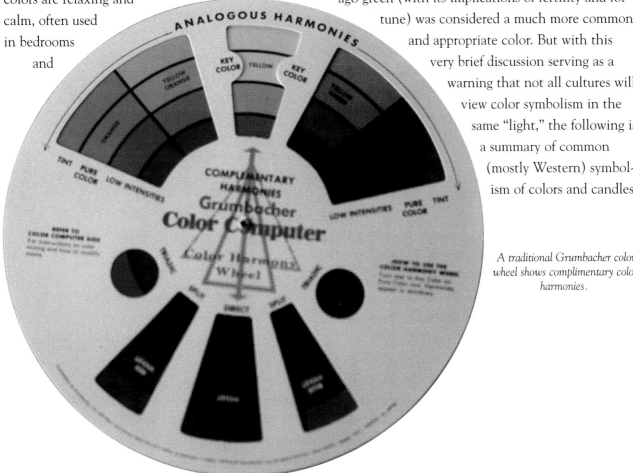

A traditional Grumbacher color wheel shows complimentary color harmonies.

Black is somewhat contradictorily a sign of evil, loss, and confusion, though at the same time representing protection, career, and contemplation. Black is associated with Saturday and is harmonious in north rooms.

Yellow represents knowledge and wisdom, intellect, charm, confidence, and persuasion as well as health, gaiety, and balance. Yellow is often used to represent the birth of a child without reference to gender. Yellow is associated with Sunday and is harmonious with central, southwest, or northeast rooms.

Gold, an obvious variant of yellow, also represents attraction, persuasion, charm, and confidence. Gold is said to be harmonious in west and northwest rooms.

White (in Western culture) is the sign of truth, sincerity, hope, power, purity, innocence, and children. White is associated with Monday and is harmonious with west and northwest rooms.

Red is one of the strongest colors, symbolizing strength, health, vigor, courage, passion, and sexual love. It is a traditional color of heroes and often represents fame and overcoming negative thoughts. Red is associated with Tuesday and is harmonious in south rooms.

Orange is another vibrant, energetic, and joyous color. It symbolizes creative expression, encouragement, attraction, potency, and adaptability. Orange is associated with Tuesday.

Green has long been regarded as the color of fertility, luck, family, peace, and harmony. It is calming and promotes serenity. Green is associated with Tuesday and is harmonious in east or southeast rooms.

Purple, probably due to its traditional rarity and cost, symbolizes ambition, power, and wealth. Purple is associated with Wednesday and is harmonious in southeast or northwest rooms.

Violet is the color of kings and priests and is noted as a symbol of peace and spirituality. Violet is sometimes thought to have the power to heal and transform.

Brown represents neutrality or uncertainty and hesitation. Brown is associated with Thursday.

Blue may be the richest color in terms of symbolism, since its various shades have many psychological and cultural meanings. Light blue represents tranquility, understanding, patience, truth, purity, and nobility. Dark blue can represent changeability and impulsiveness and is sometimes associated with Saturday. Aquamarine is calming and cooling and reflects creativity and artistic expression. Indigo represents the spirit of power and pure knowledge. Blues, in general, represent wisdom and are used to announce the birth of a baby boy. Blues are associated with Thursday and are harmonious in north or northeast rooms.

Pink represents honor, morality, success, spiritual force, unconditional love, and marriage. Pink is used to announce the birth of baby girls. Pink is associated with Friday and is harmonious in southwest rooms.

Silver and gray are associated with neutrality and stalemate. They are good colors to represent peace without concession.

Greenish-yellow or chartreuse is a symbol of anger, jealousy, cowardice, and discord.

Symbolism aside, a number of studies have shown that men and women have different color preferences. Men are said to prefer blue to red, while women prefer red to blue. Similarly men prefer orange to yellow while women prefer yellow to orange. And a majority of both men and women prefer cool colors to warm colors. That aside, it's all a matter of personal taste and preference. If you are not trying to make a symbolic gesture or statement, but are trying to select the right color for a gift, consider the color schemes favored by the recipient. Identify the main colors used in decorating a room, and select a color based on one of the following:

Triad colors are colors that are equidistant on the color wheel. The use of color triads gives a balanced color scheme—the colors don't clash. Red-violet, yellow-orange, and blue-green is a color triad as is the three primary colors.

Analogous colors are colors that are adjacent on the color wheel. These colors give little color contrast but do harmonize and are perhaps more suitable for the conservative recipient. Green, blue-green, and blue is an example of analogous colors.

Complementary colors are exact opposites on the color wheel and go well together, though giving high color contrast. Consider these colors for the vivacious, expressive recipient. Red and green, yellow-orange and blue-violet, and purple and yellow are three sets of complementary colors.

Split complementary colors are those almost opposite on the color wheel (just adjacent to the true complements). Split complements go well together but give slightly less color contrast. Red-orange, green, and blue, or green, red-violet, and red-orange are sets of split complementary colors.

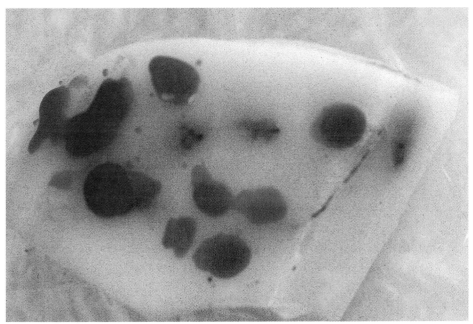

Spots of colored wax on a plain white wax remnant represent work to match a particular shade. We have found the use of a white wax block to be very convenient in developing or judging small variations in the color of waxes. It is almost impossible to judge the exact color of a candle based on the color of the molten wax. Pre-production color trial runs are essential for successful matching.

CHAPTER 13
Fragrance Blending

California lemons by our kitchen door.

Fragrance blending may be done with essential oils to create therapeutic synergies—blends that have a more pronounced effect than the individual oils. With synergies, the purpose is not necessarily to produce a balanced aroma, though most hold that the combination should be appealing. (A repugnant essential oil is thought to be less likely to have a beneficial effect. Repulsion may be the body's way of saying "no thank you, I don't need it.") However, when essential or fragrance oils and chemicals are blended to make a round, full-bodied, appealing fragrance, there are several rules of thumb that can be followed.

Blending fragrance components with what are called high, middle, and top notes normally produces pleasing fragrances. The notes describe the character of the fragrance from high, sharp, usually rather fleeting top notes to heavy, long-lasting-type base notes. Middle notes may have elements of both and are then called bridging fragrances, or they may truly be intermediate in character. Fragrances that are deep and especially long lasting are often used as fixatives—fragrance components whose main purpose is to anchor the blend and make it last longer. Fixatives are not always highly fragrant; they are almost always low notes.

In producing a blended fragrance, it is important to assemble not only the right components but to assemble them in the right ratios. The only way to check the fragrance properties of a blend is to mix the fragrances and smell them. However, fragrance chemicals are typically expensive and few want to produce ounces of blends to see if they "work." The way to evaluate them is to put a drop of an oil on a cotton swab or similar device. Then combine swabs with the desired scents. If you want to try three parts of one oil and one part of another, use three swabs of one and one of the other. But fragrances change over time. They age, sometimes mellow, and sometimes become less desirable. To do a complete evaluation, put the scented swabs together and check the blended fragrance. Put them in a single plastic bag for at least a few hours, preferably overnight. Then open the bag and smell the blend. If you like it, you have your fragrance; otherwise make some adjustments or start over.

Fragrances are also usually characterized by some designation such as floral, citrus, woodsy or animal (usually musky), or exotic. Good fragrance blends usually have themes, just like music. So a blend may be predominately floral or exotic, but with a minor theme from one of the other types. The table in Appendix III tries to give an overview of the most often used essential and fragrance oils. It presents information on the nature of the aroma (type, strength, and notes), cost, and any therapeutic benefits attributed to it. We have also tried to give a guide as to which oils may be less suitable to use by themselves in candle scents. We apologize for those who find it difficult to follow, but we have tried to summarize a lot of information in a small space.

Remember that candle fragrance oils may be produced from pure fragrance chemicals in addition to extracts and essential oils, and they may be pure blends or based in some wax-compatible solvent. Since they are proprietary, little is usually known about their exact composition, so success is not guaranteed. It is certainly easier to buy already formulated fragrance oils from a supplier, but the table in Appendix III is for those who want to try their hand at producing their own fragrances. For even more information on fragrance blending, see Robert S. McDaniel's earlier book *Essentially Soap* (Krause Publications, 2000).

CHAPTER 14
Surface Effects, Crude & Fancy

It is not economical to go to bed early to save the candles if the result is twins.

Chinese proverb

Unhappy with the candle you have just worked so hard to produce? Need a candle for a special occasion, but have only plain candles, or a candle that is the wrong color? Don't despair, there are countless things you can do to that candle to convert it from the humdrum to a unique showpiece.

There are many books that discuss sprucing up a candle with bows and ribbons or using special candleholders and displays. You can wrap almost anything around a candle; just make sure it doesn't burn when the candle is lit. And there are several ways to attach things to a candle. The obvious method is to get pin-type studs, available in many shapes at your hobby shop, and simply stick them in the candle. (Even upholstery tacks will work.) Get a nice contrasting color or a significant object to announce a birth, birthday, or emotion, and stick them into the candle.

Mottling effects

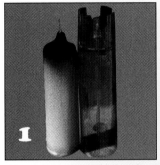

Almost any wax-soluble liquid will create mottling if it is added above the solubility limit of the wax, which is usually about 1.5%. This thoroughly-mottled candle was prepared using about 2% fragrance oil.

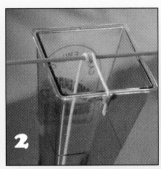

The preparation of mottled candles is no different that the preparation of any other candle. Shown here is an acrylic mold and wick waiting for the wax.

Molten, blue candle wax with liquid mottling agent (mineral oil). At this stage, it is impossible to tell that the candle will mottle.

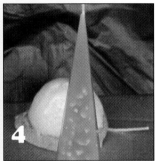

Mottled candle, freshly removed from the mold. Mottling typically occurs after the initial solidification of the paraffin—you can literally watch the starbursts form.

There are surface effects that need to be designed into the candle from the start, such as mottling. Other effects can be added to the candle at any time after it is made, such as the application of surface colors and designs. Finally, some effects, such as a crackled or fractured look, may either be designed into the candle or produced later.

Mottling occurs when a sparingly soluble additive is forced out of the wax during cooling and solidification. Mineral oil is the most common mottling agent, though essential oils, some fragrance oils, solid fatty alcohols, and even jojoba oil or wax may be used as mottling agents. The "trick" is that paraffin will normally tolerate or dissolve about 1.5% of an oil. Above that level, additives will come out of solution during cooling and create the starburst effect. About the only materials that will not cause mottling are the various polymer additives (gloss, opaque, Vybar, etc.) and stearic acid. These materials do not cause mottling because they co-crystallize with the paraffin, forming something like a hybrid crystal. Although starburst shapes are typical of mottling agents, solid mottling agents will occasionally form crescent-moon shaped defects.

Crackled effects

1 This crackled effect was created by taking a freshly-poured, warm (but solid) pillar candle and placing it in the freezer. Freshly-solidified wax has not yet had a chance to crystallize, so freezing creates stresses that can only be relieved by the formation of cracks.

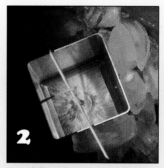

2 Pre-chilling the candle mold in ice is another often-mentioned method for making a fractured candle. A 3" aluminum mold is used here.

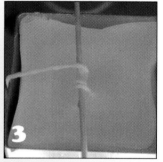

3 Unfortunately, in our experience pre-chilling has produced some unexpected and undesirable results. In this case, the candle has actually distorted and shrunk away from the sides of the mold. There was even a hole farther down in the mold that resulted as the wax shrank into the core. For this reason, we prefer the effects obtained by chilling a newly solidified candle.

Crackling, crazing, or fracturing can be either designed into a candle or added later. Crackling is somewhat related to mottling in nature. It is caused from stresses induced in the candle during the crystallization of the wax. Most candles, if removed from the mold while warm and rapidly chilled in the refrigerator or freezer will fracture.

Dipping the wax into a brittle wax composition will add a fractured effect long after a candle is made. If the newly-coated candle is placed in the refrigerator or freezer, the wax coating will fracture.

There are many ways to add surface color to a candle.

Powdered effects

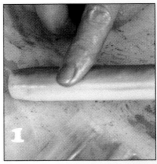

1

Gold or bronze powder is transforming a plain, commercial,
white taper into something much
more striking.

2

A finished gold taper.

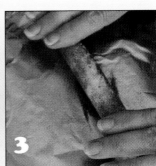

3

Rolling a white taper into a red,
pearlescent powder.

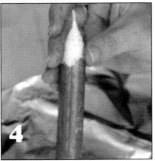

4

The powder did not produce a
uniform coating. This is partly
due to the coarseness of this color.
Heating the candle gently will
increase the color's uniformity.

Metallic surface effects can be obtained using pearlescent polyester powders. These powders are available in a range of metallic and primary colors and are simply rubbed into the candle using your finger. Fine powders such as the gold or brass colors may be applied directly, while more coarse colors may require heating the candle (with a hairdryer) to slightly soften the wax and make it more receptive to the powder.

Molten wax can be whipped as it cools, using a hand mixer or whisk to aerate the wax with a result similar to a whipped cake topping. This whipped wax can be applied like cake icing over the entire candle surface, but has the most visual impact when a dark candle burns down through a white topping, with the darker colors and lambent flame seen through the wax frosting.

You can use a stencil and paint to add a decorative touch (see page 38), use a rubber stamp and ink, or add colored wax using a *tjanting* device. You can also paint on colored wax with a wide paintbrush to add splashes of color. Within the last year or two a number of acrylic paints, developed specifically for candles, have come onto the market; they are available in most craft stores. For a more homey or rustic look, overdipping techniques can give remarkable effects.

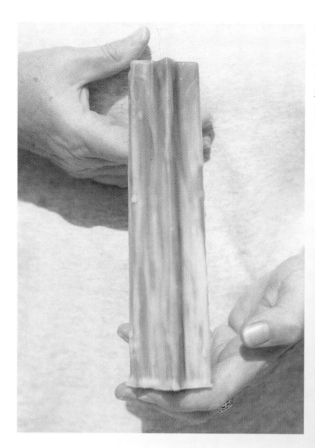

This star-shaped pillar candle was enhanced on the surface by pouring white wax over the finished candle with a spoon. Snow or frost was the desired effect. The surface is uneven and textured like drifted snow.

This white pillar candle was dipped into a neon-blue pigmented wax.

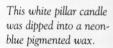

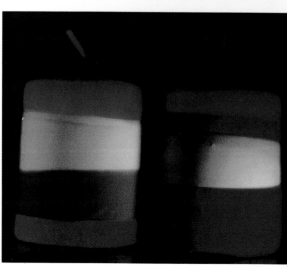

Candles coated with brightly-colored, neon pigments have the added feature of glowing under black light conditions. (A must for every teenager's room!)

Overdipping is as simple as it sounds. A colored wax, usually pigmented for intensity, is prepared in a dip tank (melted and colored) and a previously-made candle is dipped into the molten wax by holding the candle by the wick. The entire candle may be coated by total immersion, or it may be coated in stages to produce a striped effect.

Another interesting technique adds small amounts of colored wax to the surface. To do this, melt the colored wax in a small container of water. The water should be just below boiling or the agitation of the boiling water will mix the colors. Next, the candle is grasped by the wick and twisted to "wind up" the wick slightly. Then the candle is briefly plunged into the hot water, and the wax transfers to the candle surface. Since the layer is necessarily pale, the effect is normally quite pale, though if water-insoluble dye is used instead of colored wax, the effect can be intensified.

Flat objects such as flower petals may be added to the surface using a little wax as glue (see page 38). Larger objects, such as wax flower buds or almost any decorative piece of wax may be applied using *tacky wax*, a microcrystalline wax that is very sticky and will adhere to almost any wax surface. This wax is used both for the addition of decorative wax pieces and for sticking a taper into a holder or hurricane shell.

Dipped pillars

For this pillar candle, two colors were used on the water's surface, and the candle was spun slightly as it was dipped.

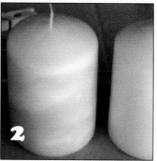

The pastel effect shown here can be darkened either by using a darker colored wax or floating a water-insoluble dye.

However, decorations only go so far, especially in transforming that strange-looking beast with the wick. If you have a dented or banged up candle, or simply are looking for a rustic look, you can make the surface uniformly non-uniform and hence very rustic using a wide variety of techniques.

Commonly used techniques to alter the candle surface include the use of a heated fork to apply a cross hatch embossed pattern; the use of a large threaded piece of metal pipe to produce a grooved surface (by turning the candle against the grooves), or the use of a hammer to dent the surface. Remember that one dent is deformation, but a surface covered with them is a customized work of art. These processes are good ways to vent frustrations, but try not to get carried away and reduce the candle to powder. If you are designing a candle for the dented effect, try to avoid the more brittle wax compositions, which can shatter if struck with too much force.

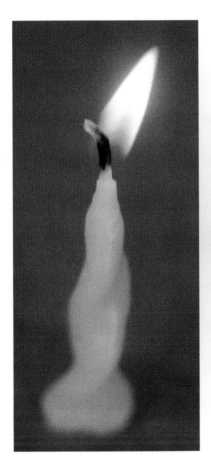

Hand dipped and twisted birthday candle. Tiny tapers are dipped exactly like large tapers, which are rolled flat while still warm then twisted. The same thing can be done with large tapers, though the base is usually left round in the large tapers so they can be inserted into a candleholder.

For that old taper, never hesitate to do something drastic. Although it is quite easy to flatten or twist a taper while it is freshly dipped and still warm, a hairdryer can quite effectively re-soften the wax and enable you to manage the same effects.

Letty Oates' book *Naturally Creative Candles* (Krause Publications, 1997) provides additional detail for candle embellishments.

CHAPTER 15
Candlemaking FAQs

Curiosity is the wick in the candle of learning.
William A. Ward

Man has long been fascinated with fire, bringing with it heat and light. But the essence of a candle is its flame.

How can I clean the wax from my molds and utensils?

The easiest way to remove wax is to preheat your oven to 150 F, and place the molds and utensils upside down on a foil (or newspaper) lined shallow baking pan. The wax will melt and run onto the foil. Be careful with acrylic molds, since these might warp if the temperature exceeds 150 F. In this case, it is best to preheat the oven and then turn it off as you add the molds. If you need them even cleaner, use (with caution) mold cleaner liquid or mineral oil.

What does it mean when a recipe calls for 1% or 0.5% of an additive?

Percent or "%" means parts per hundred. The easiest way to figure out how much to use is to first calculate the amount of wax needed for your candle. If you are going to need, for instance, 450 grams of wax (about a pound) then 1% of an additive is about 4.5 grams (the total wax needed divided by 100). Half of 1%, or 0.5%, is half of the above, or 2.25 grams. Most additive suppliers will also tell you about how much to use by volume (e.g. in teaspoons or tablespoons) for a pound of wax to get that 1% level.

Don't low melting waxes contain more oil than higher melting waxes?

Unless the wax you buy is specifically labeled as a blend, low melting (125 F) container waxes have less than 2% oil, the same order of magnitude as the higher melting (145 F) waxes.

If lower melting waxes don't contain oil, what makes them lower melting?

Basically the melting point of a wax is determined by its molecular weight. The higher melting waxes are simply bigger, longer, and heavier on the molecular level than the lower melting types.

I have purchased 145 F melting point wax for my pillars; can I use this for container candles?

The answer is yes and no. No, 145 F wax generally won't give you satisfactory results, when used by itself in a container candle. However, yes it can be used, if you add petroleum jelly to reduce the melting point.

How long can I burn a candle?

The normal rule of thumb is one hour per inch of candle diameter. So you can burn a 3" pillar for three hours. Presumably this recommendation is to prevent heat build up in the rest of the candle, which can soften the entire candle to an undesired degree.

I want to make a 12" tall candle but only have a 6" tall mold. Is there any way to use what I have?

Yes. Pour some wax (colored and scented as desired) about 1/8" thick onto a foil lined cookie sheet. Cut it into 12" long strips that fit into the mold you have. Bundle these strips in the mold, placing the wick in the center, and pour molten wax (around the strips) to fill the mold. This can be quite attractive if the strips have one or more colors different from the wax you pour into the mold.

I can't find wick sealer, what do I do?

There are several alternatives that may work for you. I have often used a tacky substance sold for attaching paper or light pictures to a wall. That rope-like, tacky, weather-stripping material may also work for you, as should florist's putty.

Can I use crayons to color my candles?

This is not recommended, since most crayons use pigment for their color and pigments tend to clog the wick and interfere with burning. If you wanted to use a crayon to make a colored outer shell for your candle, we suppose that would be viable, since pigments are often used for this purpose.

My candle has crazed or cracked. What went wrong?

This effect typically results from cooling the freshly-poured candle too fast, usually by refrigerating or freezing it as the mold cools. If you are using acrylic molds, pour the candles at the right temperature and let them cool naturally. If you are using metal molds, you may need to place them in a warm water bath to slow down the cooling rate.

I can't get my candle out of the mold. What do I do, and how do I prevent this in the future?

That is almost too broad a question. Candles with more than 10-15% beeswax need stearic acid or a mold release added while you are making the candle, unless you are using polyurethane molds. On the other hand, you can try to put the cooled candle in the freezer. This will ordinarily cause the wax to shrink away from the mold and make release easier, though in some cases the wax may crack.

Sticking can also occur if you overfill the candle when you repour to fill in the shrinkage crater. The new wax can get between the old wax and the sides of the mold, making removal a real pain. Be careful to avoid adding too much wax when you repour.

I repoured my pillar to fill in that shrinkage crater, but when I took the candle out of the mold, the new layer popped out of the candle. What happened?

You didn't heat the wax hot enough for the repour. It must be hot enough to melt the surrounding wax and to form a plug that penetrates into the wax from the original pour. It is also a good idea to prepare the cool wax surface by poking holes in the surface to let the new, molten wax penetrate. In some cases, you might actually find that the wax surface has solidified over an air pocket, and poking a hole will enable the hot wax to completely fill the voids.

I seem to have trapped air bubbles in the candle. What is the problem?

Air can get trapped in the wax if you pour it too vigorously. The remedies are to use Vybar or stearic acid—which are supposed to help minimize this problem—and to make sure your wax temperature is at the recommended temperature for the mold used. When wax is poured at cool temperatures, it is viscous and thus it is harder for the air to rise to the surface.

I made a beautiful, red candle, but it has faded over time. What happened?

Candle dyes are not light stable by themselves. When exposed to sunlight, they tend to fade, unless you add a UV absorber. You can purchase two absorbers, which must be blended (called UV-A and UV-B absorbers), or an absorber that works on both A and B wavelengths. The absorbers that work on both wavelengths are usually not as efficient as adding two.

I made a nice candle, but when I burned it, it burned straight down and left a wide rim. Why did it do this?

In order to completely burn a pillar candle, the melting point of the wax and the wick size need to be matched for optimum burning performance. It sounds as if your wax was too hard, or the wick was too small for the candle. This resulted in a small flame that did not liquefy the entire surface.

My candle sputters when I try to use it. What is wrong?

Sounds like you may have gotten water in the wick or possibly in the wax. Don't extinguish a candle by dropping water on the flame. If you used a water bath to help cool down the candle in the mold, it is possible that you had a leak that either wet the wick or enabled water to get trapped in with the wax.

My candle smokes when I burn it. What is causing this?

There are several possibilities. It could result from having too much oil in the candle or from having a wick that is too large. It is also possible that your wick is too long and needs to be trimmed.

My candle feels oily; what is wrong?

It sounds like you have oil (fragrance or mottling oil) oozing out of the candle. Use less oil in the future. If you want to save this candle, use it as a center in a larger mold and pour a larger layer around it, with little or no oil.

I made a gel candle, but the whole surface caught on fire when I tried to burn it; what is wrong?

This sounds like your candle has too low a flash point. This can happen if the mineral oil you use has a low flash point, or if you add too much fragrance oil that has a low flash point. The solution is to use the right grade (high flash point) of mineral oil and to be cautious about the type and amount of fragrance oil to use. You can also perform a test to make sure the fragrance oil is soluble in the gel. If you add several drops of fragrance to a small amount of mineral oil, the fragrance should dissolve. If it doesn't, the fragrance may not be suitable for use in gels.

My gel candle has a lot of tiny bubbles in it, but I wanted a completely clear candle. How do I prevent this?

The reason that air gets trapped is usually because the liquid gel is too viscous when you are pouring the candle. The solution is either to pour at a hotter temperature (which will give you a lower viscosity) or use less polymer to make the gel.

What are the dangers involved with gel candles?

Gel candles burn with a much hotter flame than regular container candles, so you need a good melt pool to continuously supply cooler oil to the pool and prevent overheating the container. If the blend of mineral oil and fragrance oil has too low a flash point, then you can ignite the entire surface of the candle. As with any container candle, be sure you use a tabbed wick to prevent the wick from toppling over during use.

I am trying to make aromatherapy candles, but I can't seem to get enough fragrance when I burn the candles. What can I do?

That is a great question, with no simple answer. In order to increase the scent, you add more essential oil to the candle; but to keep the oil from oozing out to the surface you add Vybar. Too much Vybar may actually bind the oil too tightly and prevent full development of the aroma.

You could also try using soy wax or tallow instead of paraffin, since the solubility of essential oils is much higher in these materials.

It is also a good idea, whatever your approach, to tightly wrap your candle as soon as it is made, to prevent evaporative loss of fragrance. Plastic wrap, shrink wrap, or even a Ziploc® bag.

Can I make container candles out of clay flowerpots?

First of all you need a flowerpot that has no bottom hole, or your wax will ultimately leak out of the bottom, creating a hazardous mess. That said, for safety reasons, you should glaze the inside of the pot to prevent wax absorption into the pores of the clay—which could ignite and turn your container candle into a torch. Waterglass (a water-based solution of sodium silicate) can be used to glaze the inside of the pot. Essentially, you need a non-porous coating that will not ignite.

Is there anything else I should consider about candle safety?

Never leave a burning candle unattended. Always have a candle sitting in a saucer or dish that will protect the surface underneath from damage by heat or contact with the wax. Even container candles can get hot enough to burn the surface they are sitting upon. Be cautious about moving lit container candles; the glass surface can get hot enough to cause burns. Don't burn a candle close to or under any sort of flammable fabric, drapery, or lampshade, etc.

I made a layered candle, but the layers seem to be trying to separate. What did I do wrong?

Either the first pour was allowed to cool too much or the second layer was not hot enough when it was poured (or both). The addition of a little microcrystalline wax (2-5%) will often prevent this occurrence. The use of micro wax can allow you to pour at cooler temperatures (to avoid color mixing), while still getting the layers to stick together.

What sort of additives can I use to improve my container candles?

Ordinarily stearic acid and other additives that increase the melting point of the candle are not desirable additives in container candles. That leaves Vybar 260 or some of the lower melting micros that give a smoother surface to the container candles.

On the other hand, if you are trying to produce a mottled container candle, you can use solid mottling agents to produce this effect in container candles, just as in pillar candles.

Can I make a container candle out of beeswax?

The answer is definitely maybe. Since beeswax is high melting, you would have to add a lot of petroleum jelly to reduce the melting point enough to produce a reasonable container candle. It can be done, but it is an expensive way to make one. It would be easier to use a container fill and look for honey fragrance oil.

What do I do with leftover wax?

Fortunately wax does not go bad, so it can be remelted and used at a later time. In fact, it is often possible to buy inexpensive, colored wax from suppliers who make it for large candle companies and sell their leftovers at bargain prices. You can use leftover colors either for making layered candles or by blending the leftovers together to make color blends. Don't try to blend too many colors in one batch, or you will end up with a lot of brownish or almost black wax. You can do the same thing with candles you don't like—just heat them up and remelt the wax.

The wax I have melts at 145 F, but someone told me I need to pour it at 120 F. How can this be?

In this specific case I cannot be sure if this is possible, but in general there is a difference between the melting point of a wax and its congealing point—the temperature at which, on cooling, the wax turns solid or ceases to flow. The congealing point is often lower than the melting point. Why? Because there is more than one process that occurs when making a candle. First the wax solidifies in a rather random, disordered state (on the molecular level). On cooling further, the wax starts to crystallize; and crystallization often occurs at a temperature about 20 F below the congealing point. When you are melting wax, though, you are melting the crystals which have a melting point different from the congealing point. The melting point is higher because it takes more energy to overcome the extra stability of the crystalline form.

How can I calculate the burn time of the candle I am making?

If you are burning the candle completely, and not leaving a shell behind, then the only way is to weigh the candle before and after burning for, say, an hour. The weight difference will give you the amount of wax burned every hour. If you divide this weight into the total weight of the fresh candle, that will give you a good estimate of the number of total hours the candle will burn.

Of course you can estimate the burn time by checking a table (see page 114). Wick manufacturers usually know how much wax, combined with a certain wick size, will be consumed per hour of burning. The difficulty arises in figuring out how your wax or wax blends compare to the blend they used to calibrate their burn times.

I know that some essential oils are dangerous to use in direct contact with the skin; can I use these oils in a candle?

In general the answer will be yes. Some oils are phototoxic, causing skin reactions if used just before going out into the sun. This is not a problem with the scent given off by a candle. Some essential oils are not recommended for use by pregnant women; although this (may or) may not be an issue with candle scent, it is best to err on the side of caution.

Is it possible to add too much of the various plastic additives to a candle?

Yes, you can add too much of almost any additive. For instance, too much Vybar or microcrystalline wax will diminish the scent by holding on too tightly to the fragrance oil. Too much fragrance oil may cause a mottled or starburst appearance on the surface. You can also add too much EVA or polyethylene (PET) polymer, and in this case it may make your candle burn irregularly or even self-extinguish.

Stearic acid may be the one additive that you can use in large amounts, say up to 30 percent or so, but in most cases that high amount adds little except cost. And if you add too much additive to increase the hardness and melting point of the candle, you may end up with an undersized wick unless you compensate by switching to a larger wick. In general you want the least amount of any additive that gets the job done.

For large diameter candles, is it better to increase the size of the wick or to switch to multiple wicks?

That's a tough question and ultimately is a matter of judgment. At some point a large wick makes your candle look more like a torch than a candle. Generally round candles at a diameter at or above about 6" will benefit from multiple wicks. And loaf candles will not burn evenly unless they are made with multiple wicks. (See page 72 for multiple wick instructions.)

Is there a way I can make a candle and add the wick later?

Of course, in fact many candles used to be made just that way. In this case you have to drill a small hole, insert the wick, and then add a little wax to fill up the space around the wick. Remember to make the hole larger than the wick you are going to use and use a metal-core wick to give it more stiffness, as you are trying to thread it through the candle. Although you can use a hand held drill, a drill press will give you much more control and better results.

You can also use granulated wax to make a container candle and insert a wick at any time.

I want to produce a starburst-type surface effect on my pillar candles, how do I do this?

The proliferation of tiny starbursts is usually called mottling. You can add mineral oil (sometimes called snowflake oil), jojoba oil, or solid mottling agents to the candle. Do not use Vybar in this case. Low levels of stearic acid, up to 2%, may enhance the mottling while serving to harden the candle (see page 99).

APPENDIX I
Mold Capacity

Round or Cylindrical Molds*

Weight in grams/ounces

Height In.		2	2	3	3	4	4	5	5	6	6	8	8	10	10	12	12
	cm.	5.1	5.1	7.6	7.6	10.2	10.2	12.7	12.7	15.2	15.2	20.3	20.3	25.4	25.4	30.5	30.5
Diameter																	
inches	cm.	g	oz.	g	oz.	g	oz.	g	oz.	g	oz.	g	oz.	g	oz.	g	oz.
1.5	3.8	46	1.6	69	2.5	93	3.3	116	4.1	139	4.9	185	6.5	232	8.2	278	9.8
2	5.1	82	2.9	124	4.4	165	5.8	206	7.3	247	8.7	329	11.6	412	14.5	494	17.4
3	7.6	185	6.5	278	9.8	371	13.1	463	16.3	556	19.6	741	26.1	927	32.7	1112	39.2
4	10.2	329	11.6	494	17.4	659	23.2	824	29.1	988	34.9	1318	46.5	1647	58.1	1977	69.7
5	12.7	515	18.2	772	27.2	1030	36.3	1287	45.4	1544	54.5	2059	72.6	2574	90.8	3089	109.0
6	15.2	741	26.1	1112	39.2	1483	52.3	1853	65.4	2224	78.4	2965	104.6	3707	130.7	4448	156.9
8	20.3	1318	46.5	1977	69.7	2636	93.0	3295	116.2	3954	139.5	5272	186.0	6590	232.4	7908	278.9
10	25.4	2059	72.6	3089	109.0	4119	145.3	5148	181.6	6178	217.9	8237	290.6	10296	363.2	12356	435.8
12	30.5	2965	104.6	4448	156.9	5931	209.2	7413	261.5	8896	313.8	11861	418.4	14827	523.0	17792	627.6

Square Pillar Molds*

Weight in grams/ounces

Height In.		2	2	3	3	4	4	5	5	6	6	8	8	10	10	12	12
	cm.	5.1	5.1	7.6	7.6	10.2	10.2	12.7	12.7	15.2	15.2	20.3	20.3	25.4	25.4	30.5	30.5
Side length																	
inches	cm.	g	oz.	g	oz.	g	oz.	g	oz.	g	oz.	g	oz.	g	oz.	g	oz.
2	5.1	105	3.7	157	5.5	236	8.3	295	10.4	354	12.5	472	16.6	590	20.8	708	25.0
3	7.6	236	8.3	398	14.0	531	18.7	664	23.4	796	28.1	1062	37.5	1327	46.8	1593	56.2
4	10.2	472	16.6	708	25.0	944	33.3	1180	41.6	1416	49.9	1888	66.6	2360	83.2	2832	99.9
5	12.7	737	26.0	1106	39.0	1475	52.0	1844	65.0	2212	78.0	2950	104.0	3687	130.1	4425	156.1
6	15.2	1062	37.5	1593	56.2	2124	74.9	2655	93.6	3186	112.4	4248	149.8	5309	187.3	6371	224.7

Oval Molds*

Weight in grams/ounces

Height In.	2	2	3	3	4	4	5	5	6	6	8	8	10	10	12	12
cm.	5.1	5.1	7.6	7.6	10.2	10.2	12.7	12.7	15.2	15.2	20.3	20.3	25.4	25.4	30.5	30.5

Circumference

inches	cm.	g	oz.	g	oz.	g	oz.	g	oz.	g	oz.	g	oz.	g	oz.	g	oz.
3	7.6	19	0.7	28	1.0	38	1.3	47	1.7	56	2.0	75	2.6	94	3.3	113	4.0
4	10.2	33	1.2	50	1.8	67	2.4	83	2.9	100	3.5	134	4.7	167	5.9	200	7.1
5	12.7	52	1.8	78	2.8	104	3.7	130	4.6	156	5.5	209	7.4	261	9.2	313	11.0
6	15.2	75	2.6	113	4.0	150	5.3	188	6.6	225	7.9	300	10.6	376	13.2	451	15.9
7	17.8	102	3.6	153	5.4	204	7.2	256	9.0	307	10.8	409	14.4	511	18.0	613	21.6
8	20.3	134	4.7	200	7.1	267	9.4	334	11.8	401	14.1	534	18.8	668	23.6	801	28.3
9	22.9	169	6.0	254	8.9	338	11.9	423	14.9	507	17.9	676	23.8	845	29.8	1014	35.8
10	25.4	209	7.4	313	11.0	417	14.7	522	18.4	626	22.1	835	29.4	1043	36.8	1252	44.2
12	30.5	300	10.6	451	15.9	601	21.2	751	26.5	901	31.8	1202	42.4	1502	53.0	1803	63.6
14	35.6	409	14.4	613	21.6	818	28.9	1022	36.1	1227	43.3	1636	57.7	2045	72.1	2454	86.6
16	40.6	534	18.8	801	28.3	1068	37.7	1335	47.1	1602	56.5	2137	75.4	2671	94.2	3205	113.0
18	45.7	676	23.8	1014	35.8	1352	47.7	1690	59.6	2028	71.5	2704	95.4	3380	119.2	4056	143.1
20	50.8	835	29.4	1252	44.2	1669	58.9	2086	73.6	2504	88.3	3338	117.8	4173	147.2	5008	176.6

Conical Molds*

Weight in grams/ounces

Height In.	2	2	3	3	4	4	5	5	6	6	8	8	10	10	12	12
cm.	5.1	5.1	7.6	7.6	10.2	10.2	12.7	12.7	15.2	15.2	20.3	20.3	25.4	25.4	30.5	30.5

Base diameter

inches	cm.	g	oz.	g	oz.	g	oz.	g	oz.	g	oz.	g	oz.	g	oz.	g	oz.
1.5	3.8	15	0.5	23	0.8	31	1.1	39	1.4	46	1.6	62	2.2	77	2.7	93	3.3
2	5.1	27	1.0	41	1.5	55	1.9	69	2.4	82	2.9	110	3.9	137	4.8	165	5.8
3	7.6	62	2.2	93	3.3	124	4.4	154	5.4	185	6.5	247	8.7	309	10.9	371	13.1
4	10.2	110	3.9	165	5.8	220	7.7	275	9.7	329	11.6	439	15.5	549	19.4	659	23.2
5	12.7	172	6.1	257	9.1	343	12.1	429	15.1	515	18.2	686	24.2	858	30.3	1030	36.3
6	15.2	247	8.7	371	13.1	494	17.4	618	21.8	741	26.1	988	34.9	1236	43.6	1483	52.3

Pyramidal Molds (square base)*

Weight in Grams

Height In.	2	2	3	3	4	4	5	5	6	6	8	8	10	10	12	12
cm.	5.1	5.1	7.6	7.6	10.2	10.2	12.7	12.7	15.2	15.2	20.3	20.3	25.4	25.4	30.5	30.5

Base side

inches	cm.	g	oz.	g	oz.	g	oz.	g	oz.	g	oz.	g	oz.	g	oz.	g	oz.
1.5	3.8	20	0.7	29	1.0	39	1.4	49	1.7	59	2.1	79	2.8	98	3.5	118	4.2
2	5.1	35	1.2	52	1.8	70	2.5	87	3.1	105	3.7	140	4.9	175	6.2	210	7.4
3	7.6	79	2.8	118	4.2	157	5.5	197	6.9	236	8.3	315	11.1	393	13.9	472	16.6
4	10.2	140	4.9	210	7.4	280	9.9	350	12.3	420	14.8	559	19.7	699	24.7	839	29.6
5	12.7	218	7.7	328	11.6	437	15.4	546	19.3	655	23.1	874	30.8	1092	38.5	1311	46.2
6	15.2	315	11.1	472	16.6	629	22.2	787	27.7	944	33.3	1259	44.4	1573	55.5	1888	66.6

★ The above weights are listed for paraffin wax. Beeswax will require approximately 10% more wax.

APPENDIX II
Wick Selection Guides

The following tables are meant as a guide to wick selection for specific applications. The best wick for the purpose, however, must be demonstrated in use, since no general summary can accurately reflect all possible combinations of waxes and additives. Although many different size or numbering systems exist, we selected the most common system in use. If the data do not reflect your experience, compare the number of feet per pound. That is a more accurate measure of size. The data and recommended applications are compiled from many sources including wick manufacturers and various retailers. As such, these tables should be viewed as starting points rather than the definitive word on what to use in a given candle.

Flat Braid Wicks

# plies	Ft/lb.	Burn rate	Applications	
12	2670	4.3	<.75" tapers	
15	2145	5.1	<1" tapers	
18	1785	5.15	1-2" pillars	
21	1530	5.2	2-3" pillars	tapers
24	1350	5.7	2-3" pillars	tapers
27	1200	6.2	2.5-3" pillars	tapers
30	1065	6.3	3.5-4" pillars	
36	900	7.1	4-4.5" pillars	
45	720	7.2	4.5-5" pillars	
60	540	6.4	5-6" pillars	

Zinc-core wicks

Size	Ft/lb.	Burn rate	Applications
28-24	1332	1.7	sm. containers
34-24	1344	1.8	ca. 1" containers
36-24	1347	2.2	<2" containers
34-40	1011	2.3-2.7	2-3" containers
36-24-24	1101	3.1	2-3" containers
44-20-18	1029	3.3	2-3" containers
44-24-18	945	4.3	2-3.5" votives and containers
44-28-18	837	5	<4" containers
44-32-18	765	5	<4" containers
51-32-18	747	5	3-4" containers
60-44-18	642	6.6	>4" containers

Square Braid Wicks

Size	Ft/lb	Burn rate	Applications	
#6/0	2520	4.6		sm. beeswax tapers
#5/0	2265	4.9		sm. beeswax tapers
#4/0	1740	5.5	<2" pillars	sm. beeswax tapers
#3/0	1500	6.1	<2.5" pillars	beeswax tapers
#2/0	1320	6	2-3" pillars	beeswax tapers
#1/0	1185	7	>3" pillars	<1.5" beeswax
#1	1080	7.3	1-2" pillars	
#2	900	7.5	2-4" pillars	1-2" beeswax
#3	750	8.1	3.5-4" pillars	<2.5" beeswax
#4	645	8.8	4-4.5" pillars	
#5	600		5-5.5" pillars	>2.5" beeswax
#6	510		5.5-6" pillars	
#10	300		lg. containers and patio lights	

$\mathcal{A}$PPENDIX III
Fragrance Blending Table

Abbreviations Used:

Abs. Absolute
Res. Resinoid
LL Long lasting
F Scent tends to fade
S Strong, dominating scent
MS Moderate scent
LS Light scent, as typically used
Fix Often used as a fixative in perfumery
Men Often used in men's fragrances
(%) Typical usage levels in perfumery; use in candles may be limited by solubility
$ Under $100 per pound, depending on volume purchased
$$ Costly; over $100 per pound at volume
$$$ Extremely costly, at or above $1,000 a pound.
Q May have solubility or compatibility issues in candles
Un Unlikely to be usable in or compatible with candles
Top Top notes
Mid Middle notes
Bas Base note

Angelica root: (Angelica archangelica) (.5-2%), MS, $$$, Q, Bas-Mid. Herbaceous, spicy aroma. Invigorating, antidepressant. Used in herbal and woodsy fragrances.

Star anise: (1-8%), MS, $, Mid. Spicy, herbaceous aroma. Relieves coughing. Used in spice, herbal, and citrus fragrances.

Aniseseed: (Pimpinella anisum) (1-8%), MS, $, Mid-Top. Spicy, herbaceous aroma (licorice). Relaxing. Once used as an aphrodisiac, a reputation that modern studies may support, since it is sensually appealing to women. Blend with bay, cedar wood, and citrus.

Basil: (Ocimum basilicum) (1-6%), MS, $, Mid-Top. Herbaceous, spicy aroma. Used to clear the head of colds and ease headache; used against melancholy and depression in the Middle Ages; used against stress and insomnia; considered an aphrodisiac by the Romans. Recommended with bergamot, clary sage, geranium, hyssop, lavender, melissa, sandalwood, and verbena.

Bay: (Pimenta acris, laurus nobilis) (1-6%), MS, $$, Q, Bas-Mid. Spicy, herbaceous aroma. A Roman symbol of wisdom and peace. Good for respiratory problems. Blends well with eucalyptus, juniper, lavender, lemon, rose, rosemary, thyme, and ylang ylang.

Bergamot: (Citrus auramias bergamia) (5-10+%), MS, $$, Top. Characteristic citrus aroma. Uplifting and invigorating oil. Blend with citrus and floral fragrances.

Calendula: (Calendula officianalis) (.2-1.5%), LL, S, $$, Top. Intoxicating, herbaceous, green, fruity aroma. Blends with florals, citrus, and herbal fragrances.

Calendula or pot marigold self-seeding annual

Camphor, white: (Cinnamon camphor) (.5-2%), F, S, $, Mid-Top. Cool, piney aroma. Used as an insect repellant and deodorant. Blends well with citrus, and mint.

Cananga: (Cananga odroata) (.5-5%), LL, MS, $, Q, Bas. Intoxicating, jasmine, orchid-like aroma. Reputed to have antidepressant effects. Use in intoxicating floral fragrances, especially with violet.

Caraway: (Apium carvi) (.5-4%), MS, $, Mid-Top. Herbaceous, spicy aroma. Blend with lavender, eucalyptus, and herbal fragrances.

Cardamon: (Elettaria cardamomum) (.3-3%), F, S, $$, Mid-Top, Men. Spicy, herbaceous aroma. One of the oldest known essential oils. Reported aphrodisiac properties. Blends with geranium, juniper, lemon, rosewood, and verbena.

Cassia: (.5-4%), LL, MS, $, Mid. Spicy aroma. Used as a room scent only. Blend same as cinnamon.

Cedar wood: (Juniperus virginiani) (1-10%), LL, LS, $, Fix, Bas-Mid, Men. Woodsy aroma. Warm, energizing fragrance. One of the oldest woods used as incense. Blends with pine, rose, rosemary, vetiver, cypress and other wood oils as well as patchouli.

Chamomile, German: (Matricaria chamomilla) (.5-4%), LL, MS, $$, Mid. Herbaceous, fruity aroma. Also called blue chamomile from the characteristic blue color of the azulene, which is formed during steam distillation. See Chamomile, Roman.

Chamomile, Roman: (Chamaemelum nobile) (.5-4%), LL, MS, $$$, Mid-Top, Men. Herbaceous, fruity aroma. Has been in continuous use from the time of the Egyptians, who dedicated it to the gods. Its name is derived from the Greek Chamaimelon, or apple on the ground, due to its strong apple scent. It is variously recommended for allergies, migraine, to ease anxiety, and treat insomnia. Blends well with angelica, geranium, lavender, lemon, palmarosa, patchouli, rose, and ylang ylang.

Cinnamon, bark: (Cinnamomum zeylanicum) (.5-5%), LL, MS, $, Bas-Mid. Spicy, woodsy aroma. Like the leaf oil, it is a comforting, refreshing room fragrance. Blends well with most citrus oils and clove.

Cinnamon, leaf: (Cinnamomum zeylanicum) (.5-5%), LL, MS, $, Bas-Mid. Spicy, herbaceous, woodsy aroma. Blends well with most citrus oils and clove.

Citronella: (Cymbopgon nardus) (.2-2%), S, $, Top. Citrus. Herbal aroma. Most noted as an insect repellant. Blends with geranium, citrus, and cedar.

Clary sage: (Salvia sclaria) (1-4%), MS, $, Mid-Top. Herbaceous, balsamic aroma. Blends well with citrus, fir, and lavender. It was considered (16th century) to be an aphrodisiac. Its name is from the Latin clarus for its use to relieve tired, sore eyes. It is also used to combat general fatigue and depression. An ancient Latin saying was "cur morietur homo, cui salvia crescit in horto?" Or "How can a man die who has sage growing in his garden?"

Clove bud: (Eugenia caryophyllata) (.3-3%), LL, MS, $, Q, Mid-Top. Spicy aroma. The name is from the Latin clavus, nail shaped. Medicinal history dates to Greeks, Romans, and Chinese. Used to strengthen memory, lift depression. Blends with basil, cinnamon, lemon, nutmeg, orange, and rosemary.

Clove leaf: (Eugenia caryophyllata) (.5-4%), LL, MS, $, Q, Mid-Top. Spicy, herbaceous aroma. Similar composition to the bud oil.

Coriander: (Coriandrum sativum) (1-7%), MS, $, Top. Spicy, chemical, herbaceous aroma.

Cumin seed: (Cuminum cyminum) (.1-.3%), F, S, $$, Q, Mid, Men. Green, animal, herbaceous aroma. Stimulating, invigorating, both mentally and physically. Blends with citrus and woodsy fragrances.

Elemi gum: (Canarium luzonicum) (1-9%), LS, $, Fix, Top. Citrus, balsamic aroma. Said to stimulate the immune system, some applications for asthma and insomnia.

Eucalyptus G.: (Eucalyptus globulous) (.5-3%), F, S, $, Top. Cool, herbaceous aroma. Used as an insect repellent and for pulmonary conditions. Blends with coriander, juniper, lavender, lemongrass, melissa, and thyme.

Eucalyptus Cit.: (Eucalyptus citriodora) (.5-3%), F, S, $, Q, Top. Citrus, herbaceous, balsamic aroma. Similar pulmonary effects to globulous, but much milder and hence safer, known as lemon eucalyptus. Blends with other citrus fragrances.

Fennel: (Foenculum vulgare) (.5-5%), MS, $, Mid-Top. Spicy. Orchid-like aroma. Once thought to be an aphrodisiac, energizing. Blends with herbals and florals.

Geranium: (Pelargonium graveolens) (.5-5%), MS, $, Bas-Mid. Rose-like aroma. Relieves stress. Blends well with lavender, rose, patchouli, basil, bay, sage, lavender, rosemary, and sandalwood. Pelargonium is derived from the Greek for stork's bill, reflecting the fruit's shape. 300-500 pounds of plant material are required to produce a single pound of essential oil.

Ginger: (Zingiber officianlae) (1-10%), MS, $, Top. Spicy, herbaceous, woodsy aroma. An energizing oil. Use for spice top notes.

Grapefruit: (Citrus decumana) (1-8%), F, MS, $, Top. Citrus aroma. Refreshing, uplifting fragrance. Use in blends for fresh citrus top notes.

Guaiacwood: (Bulnesia sarmienti) (1-9%), LL, LS, $, Q, Bas, Men. Rosy, woodsy, slightly smoky aroma. Often used with rose or similar fragrances (also with citrus).

Orris, Abs: (Iris pallidia) (1-5%), MS, $$$, Fix, Mid. Iris aroma. Fixative, especially in florals.

One of many species of jasmine, easily cultivated in southern California.

Jasmine, Abs: (Jasminum officinale) (1-5%), LL, MS, $$$, Bas. Iris aroma. Warm, uplifting, sensuous, floral fragrance, called the "king of perfumes or flower oils," with soothing and calming properties. Blends with mandarin, lavender, and rose.

Juniper: (Juniperus communis) (.5-4%), F, MS, $, Mid-Top. Herbaceous, conifer aroma.

Juniper berry: (.5-4%), F, MS, $, Top. Herbaceous, conifer, spicy aroma. Widespread medicinal use in Tibet, Rome, Greece, and Arabia. Blends with bergamot, geranium, lemongrass, melissa, rosemary, sandalwood, and various firs.

Lavandin: (Lavandula fragrans or intermedia) (1-8%), MS, $, Mid-Top. Herbaceous, slight chemical, cool aroma. This hybrid species is a cross between true lavender and aspic, or spike lavender. Whereas lavender is calming and relaxing, lavandin is more stimulating and energizing. Blends with bergamot, chamomile, clary sage, and geranium. A single pound of essential oils is produced from approximately thirty-five pounds of flowers.

Lavender: (Lavandula angustifolia) (1-10+%), LL, MS, $, Mid. Herbaceous, slight chemical aroma. "English Lavender" from the Latin *lavare*, to wash. Romans added it to their baths for antiseptic and insect repellant properties. Traditional uses include calming nerves. A 1995 article in the *Lancet* (British Medical Journal) extols the ability of lavender to regulate sleep patterns in people who are being temporarily taken off sleep regulating medication. One of the most important essential oils, one pound of oil is produced from about one hundred pounds of flowers. Blends with bay, bergamot, chamomile, clary sage, eucalyptus, geranium, nutmeg, patchouli, thyme, and rosemary.

Lavender, spike: (Lavandula latifolia or spica, also called aspic) (1-6%), MS, $, Mid-Top. Cool, herbal, slightly chemical aroma. Like lavandin, this oil is more energizing rather than calming. Eases breathing and clears a stuffy head. Blend as with lavender.

Lemon: (Citrus Limonum) (1-8%), F, MS, $, Q, Top. Citrus aroma. Refreshing, uplifting, penetrating fragrance. Blends well with other citrus fragrances as well as spicy fragrances (clove, cinnamon, cardamom, etc.).

Lemongrass: (Cymbopogon citratus) (1-5%), MS, $, Q, Top. Citrus, herbaceous aroma. Flea and tick repellant that is also stimulating and revitalizing. Blends with basil, coriander, geranium, lavender, neroli, palmarosa, rosemary, tea tree, litsea, and cubeba.

Lime: (Citrus aurantifolia) (1-5%), F, MS, $, Top, citrus. Conifer aroma. Refreshing, uplifting fragrance. Blend for citrus (or bay) fresh top notes.

Litsea Cubeba: (Litsea cubeba) (1-5%), MS, $, Q, Top. Citrus aroma. Often added to extend the citrus aroma of other essential oils.

Mandarin: (Origanum marjorana) (1-9%), LS, $, Top. Citrus, fruity aroma. Blend for citrus-fresh top notes.

Marjoram: (Origanum marjorana) (1-6%), MS, $, Mid. Herbaceous, spicy aroma. The Greek goddess Aphrodite supposedly used marjoram to cure the wounds of her son, Aeneus. Blends with bergamot, chamomile, lavender, nutmeg, rosemary, and ylang ylang.

Menthol: (1-9%), LS, $, Top. Cooling aroma. Deodorizing, refreshing, insect repellant. Blends with lavender, rose, or geranium for minty notes.

Myrrh oil: (Commiphora myrrha) (1-7%), LL, MS, $$, Fix, Bas. Balsamic, spicy aroma. Uplifting, soothing, stress relieving fragrance. Blends with spicy and exotic fragrances.

Neroli: (Citrus aurantium) (1-8%), MS, $$$, Mid-Top. Citrus, slight chemical, intoxicating aroma. Sleep aid, relieving chronic anxiety and depression. The prohibitive expense of this essential oil is a result of the yield: It takes about one thousand pounds of flowers (from the bitter orange tree) to produce one pound of oil. Blends with bergamot, coriander, geranium, lavender, palmarosa, petitgrain, rosemary, sandalwood, and ylang ylang.

Nutmeg: (Myristica fragrans) (1-7%), MS, $, Mid. Herbaceous, spicy, citrus aroma. The oil comes from the seed kernel, mace is the husk. Stimulant. Blends with cinnamon, clove, coriander, melissa, patchouli, rosemary, and tea tree.

Olibanum: (Boswellia thurifera) (1-6%), F, LS, $$, Fix, Bas-Mid, Men. Balsamic, phenolic aroma. Olibanum means Lebanon Oil. The traditional use is to produce a calm, meditative state, ease shortness of breath, etc. It blends well with citrus, exotics, and wood fragrances such as patchouli, sandalwood, and pine.

Orange: (Citrus sinensis) (1-7%), MS, $, Top. Citrus aroma. Uplifting, soothing fragrance. Use for fresh citrus top notes

Oregano: (Thymus capitatus) (1-6%), MS, $$, Mid-Top. Herbaceous, spicy, phenolic aroma. Used to promote mental clarity and alertness, soothing. Blends with spicy, pine, and woodsy fragrances.

Orange blossoms and immature fruit.

Palmarosa: (Cymbopogon martini) (1-6%), MS, $$, Mid. Rosy, herbaceous aroma. Reputed to refresh and clarify the mind. Blends with bergamot, geranium, lavender, melissa, petitgrain, rosewood, sandalwood, and ylang ylang.

Patchouli: (Pogostemon cablin) (1-8%), LL, MS, $$, Bas-Mid. Woodsy, herbaceous aroma. Long history of medical use in Malaysia, China, India, and Japan, and equally long use as an aphrodisiac. Blends with bergamot, clary sage, geranium, lavender, lemongrass, neroli, rosewood, and peppermint.

Pepper, black: (Piper nigrum) (1-5%), MS, $$, Mid, Men. Spicy, herbaceous aroma. Like most spicy exotics, pepper has a reputation as an aphrodisiac. Blends in citrus and spicy fragrances plus sandalwood, lavender and rosemary.

Peppermint: (Mentha piperita) (.2-2%), S, $, Top-Mid. Cool, herbaceous, balsamic aroma. A very refreshing, reviving, and stimulating fragrance. According to Roman mythology, the nymph menthe (or minthe), a casualty of an ancient love triangle, was changed into the herb by Pluto. Blends with juniper, spearmint, patchouli, rosemary, lavender, and tea tree.

Peru Balsam: (Myroxylon balsamum) (2-9%), LL, LS, $, Bas. Balsamic, vanilla with hints of woodsy/spicy aroma. Strengthening fragrance. Blend into fruity and floral fragrances.

Petitgrain: (Citrus aurantium) (1-7%), MS, $, Top. Citrus, woodsy aroma. Often used in combination with neroli. One of three essential oils from the orange tree, coming from the leaves. It is reported to clear confusion, depression, and mental fatigue. Blends with bergamot, cardamom, geranium, lavender, melissa, palmarosa, rosemary, rosewood, neroli, and ylang ylang. Contains (40-80%) linalyl acetate, geraniol, geranyl acetate, and limonene.

Pimento: (Allspice, Pimenta officinalis) (.3-3%), LL, MS, $, Bas-Mid. Warm, spicy aroma. Fragrance similar to cloves. Used to relieve tiredness, exhaustion. Blends with lavender, lemongrass, and nutmeg.

Pine Needle: (Abies alba) (1-6%), MS, $, Mid, Men. Conifer, herbal aroma. Fresh, deodorizing fragrance. Blends with other pines and lilac.

Rose, otto: (Rosa damascena) (.5-5%), MS, $$$. Bridging, characteristic rose aroma. Tremendously uplifting fragrance. This is one of the oldest (and most expensive) of the essential oils, roughly 4,400 pounds of rose blossoms are needed to produce a single pound of essential oil. Myths relating to roses abound, but it is a noted symbol of silence—a rose suspended over a table was a sign that the discussions held were to be kept secret by all participants, hence the term "sub rosa," under the rose. Widely used in perfumery and cosmetics both to improve the fragrance bouquet and for the soothing properties to mind and skin. Blends with other floral oils and almost any other type of fragrance as well.

Rosemary: (Rosmarinus officinalis) (.5-5%), MS, $, Mid-Top. Herbaceous, cool, slightly chemical, woodsy aroma. "Dew of the sea," soothes the nerves and aids breathing (asthma). It has been found in the Egyptian tombs, probably as a result of its antioxdant, preservative qualities. Used by Egyptians, Greeks, and Romans. Blends with basil, geranium, lavender, lemongrass, melissa, peppermint, and tangerine.

Rosewood: (Aniba rosaeodora) (1-8%), MS, $$, Mid. Rosy, slightly chemical aroma. Similar chemical makeup to the Taiwan Ho or Shiu tree. Recommended for antidepressant and antimigraine properties. Blends well with lavender and rose geranium.

Sage: (Salvia officinalis) (1-6%), MS, $, Top. Warm, herbaceous, spicy, and slightly camphorous aroma. It quickens senses and is used with chamomile to relieve asthma attacks. Clary sage is more commonly used for Aromatherapy.

Sandalwood: (Santalum album) (1-10%), LL, LS, $$, Bas. Woodsy aroma. Noted for its uplifting and aphrodisiac properties, but has been used in religious rites for centuries, both as incense and even in the construction of temples. Fragrance reportedly builds with time, possibly with exposure to air. Blends well with rose, jasmine, lavender, patchouli, and other exotics.

Spearmint: (Mentha viridas) (.5-4%), MS, $, Mid-Top. Cool, herbal, spicy aroma. Used against headache, nausea, antidepressant, mental strain, and fatigue. Blends well with peppermint and various citrus oils.

Styrax: Res, (Liquidandbar orientalis) (1-7%), LL, MS, $, Fix, Mid. Orchid-like, spicy aroma. Mood enhancing. Blends with exotics, balsams, and spicy fragrances.

Thyme, white: (Thymus Vulgaris) (.2-1.5%), LL, $$, Q, Mid. Phenolic, herbaceous spicy aroma. It has strong antiseptic properties, due to thymol in oil. It has varied uses including the treatment of stuffy nose and fatigue. It was used by the Sumarians, Egyptians, and Romans who thought it dispelled melancholy and promoted bravery. From the Greek *Thumos* for smell or perfume. It was also carried to prevent airborne diseases. Blends with citrus, lavender, pine, and rosemary.

Vanilla: Abs, (Vanilla planifolia) (1-10+%), LL, LS, $$$, Un, Bas. Balsamic, woodsy aroma. Uplifting fragrance. Blends with florals and exotic fragrances.

Vetiver: (Andropogon zizanioides) (1-7%), LL, MS, $$, Fix, Bas. Woodsy, animal aroma. Calming and sedating. Its earthy, woody odor often mellows with age. It takes almost three hundred pounds of this grass to produce a single pound of oil.

Wintergreen: (Gualtheria promcumbens) (.3-3%) F, S, $, Q, Mid-Top. Heavy, intoxicating aroma, orchid-like, and phenolic. Used to relieve respiratory problems. Use with ylang ylang and other heavy florals.

Ylang ylang (ee-long, ee-long): (Cananga odorata) (1-7%), MS, $$, Mid. Intoxicating jasmine and orchid-like aroma. "Flower of flowers," "Queen of Perfumes" (and poor man's jasmine as well). I've found these flower buds used in both Taiwan and Thailand in strings to be hung in automobiles as natural air fresheners. In Thailand, they were strung together in long strands with rose petals and jasmine buds. Used and known for its effects as an antidepressant, antiseptic, aphrodisiac, and against insomnia and anxiety. Blends well with lavender, rosemary, and other florals.

APPENDIX IV
Suppliers

Complete Suppliers (wax, additives, equipment)

The Candlewic Company
8244 Easton Road
Ottsville, Pa. 18942
Tel: 610-847-2076
Fax: 630-847-2069
and
Naperville, Ill. 60585
Tel: 630-848-0781
Fax: 630-848-0782
waxnwic@epix.net
www.candlewic.com

The Barker Company
15106 10th Avenue Southwest
Seattle, Wash. 98166
Tel: 800-543-0601
Fax: 206-244-7334
customerservice@barkerco.com
www.barkerco.com

Pourette Manufacturing
P.O. Box 70469
Seattle, Wash. 98107
Toll free: 800-888-9425
Fax: 206-789-3640
pourette@aol.com
www.pourette.com

Yaley Enterprises
7664 Avianca Drive
Redding, Calif. 96002
Tel: 877-365-5212
Fax: 530-365-6483
info@yaley.com
www.yaley.com

Wax Manufacturers and Wholesalers

Calwax Corporation
5367 Ayon Avenue
Irwindale, Calif. 91706
Tel: 626-969-4334
Fax: 626-969-3017
information@calwax.com
www.calwax.com

C. J. Robinson
522 New Gulph Road
Haverford, Pa. 19041
Tel: 610-896-5022
Fax: 610-896-5031
wxes@cjrobinson.com
www.cjrobinson.com

Dussek Campbell Limited
Cowling Road
Chorley, Lancashire PR6 9DR
United Kingdom
Tel: +44(0) 1257 278 321
Fax: +44(0) 1257 267 398

Dussek Campbell, Inc.
3650 Touhy Avenue
Skokie, Ill. 60076
Tel: (847) 679-6300
Fax: (847) 679-6312
info@dussekwax.com
www.dussekwax.com

Dussek Campbell Ply. Limited
144-152 Fitzgerald Road, Laverton
North, Melbourne, Victoria, Australia
Tel: +61(3) 9368 0088
Fax: +61(3) 9369 6070

Moore & Munger, Inc.
Two Corporate Drive, Suite 434
Shelton, Conn. 06484
Toll free: 800-423-7071
www.mooremunger.com
wax@mooremunger.com

Polygon Corporation
200 West 2nd Street
P.O. Box 348
South Boston, Mass. 02127
Tel: 617-268-4455
Fax: 617-268-9636
www.polygonwax.com
mail@polygonwax.com
advice@polygonwax.com
questions@polygonwax.com

Strahl & Pitsch, Inc.
230 Great East Neck Rd.
West Babylon, N.Y. 11704
Tel: 631-587-9000
Fax: 631-587-9120
info@strahlpitsch.com
www.strahlpitsch.com

The International Group, Inc.
Toll free: 800-852-6537
www.igiwax.com

USA
85 Old Eagle School Road
P.O. Box 383
Wayne, Pa. 19087
Tel: 610-687-9030
Toll free: 800-852-6537
Fax: 610-254-8548

CANADA
50 Salome Drive
Agincourt, Ontario M1S 2A8
Tel: 416-293-4151
Fax: 416-293-0344
(Quebec)
650-32nd Avenue, Suite 406
Lachine, Quebec H8T 3K5
Tel: 514-634-8965
Fax: 514-636-5467

Astorlite Wax
(Corporate Headquarters)
Honeywell International Inc.
Specialty Chemicals
P.O. Box 1053
Morristown, N.J. 07962-1053
Tel: 973-455-2145
Toll Free: 800-222-0094 (Customer Service)
Fax: 973-455-6154 (Customer Service)
www.astorcorp.com

Honeywell Specialty Chemicals
Astor Corporation
1425 Oakbrook Drive, Suite 600
Norcross, Ga. 30093
Tel: 770-448-8083
Toll Free: 800-421-4929 (Customer
Service)
Fax: 770-448-5553

Strohmeyer & Arpe Company, Inc.
636 Morris Turnpike
Short Hills, N.J. 07078
Tel: 973-379-6600
Fax: 973-379-8181
sales@strohmeyer.com
www.strohmeyer.com

Koster Keunen
90 Bourne Blvd.
Sayville, N.Y. 11782
Tel: 516-589-0400
Fax: 516-589-1232
info@kosterkeunenwaxes.com
www.kosterkeunenwaxes.com

Glorybee
120 North Seneca
Eugene, Ore. 97402
Toll free: 800-GLOR-YBE
sales@glorybee.com
www.glorybee.com

Mann Lake, Ltd.
501 South 1st Street
Hackensack, Minn. 56452
Toll free: 800-880-7694
Fax: 218-675-6156
beekeepr@mannlakeltd.com
www.mannlakeltd.com

CONTAINERS

Anchor Hocking Specialty Glass
Tel: 877-643-9204 to request a catalog
Fax: 800-503-9041 (Monaca, Pa.)
information@ahsg.com
www.ahsg.com

SKS Bottle & Packaging, Inc.
3 Knabner Road
Mechanicville, N.Y. 12118
Tel: 518-899-7488
Toll free: 800-810-0440
custom@sks-bottle.com
www.sks-bottle.com

Sunburst Bottle Company
5710 Auburn Blvd, Suite 7
Sacramento, Calif. 95841
Tel: 916-348-5576
sunburst@cwo.com
www.sunburstbottle.com

Misc. Supplies

Dick Blick Art Materials
P.O. Box 1267
Galesburg, Ill. 61402-1267
Tel: 800-447-8192
Fax: 800-621-8293
www.dickblick.com

Smooth-on (mold making supplies)
2000 Saint John Street
Easton, Pa. 18042
Tel: 610-252-5800
Toll free: 800-762-0744
Fax: 610-252-6200
smoothon@smooth-on.com
www.smooth-on.com

Ricky at Luna Parc (custom decorative
pieces)
22 De Groat Road
Montague, N.J. 07827
Tel: 973-948-2160
lunaparc@aol.com
www.lunaparc.com

Atkins & Pearce, Inc. (wicks)
1 Braid Way
Covington, Ky. 41017
Tel: 859-356-2001
Toll free: 800-837-7477
or 888-APBRAID
Fax: 859-356-2395
Toll free fax: 800-550-2395
braid@braidway.com
www.braidway.com

Fragrances

Berje, Inc.
5 Lawrence Street
Bloomfield, N.J. 07003
Tel: 973-748-8980
Fax: 973-680-9618
Info@berjeinc.com
www.berjeinc.com

Chemessence
The Whitmeyer Company
4025 Glenwick Lane
Dallas, Texas 75205
Tel: 214-528-2459
www.georgew.com

Intercontinental Fragrances (wholesale
only)
10422 West Gulf Bank Road
Houston, Texas 77040
Tel: 713-896-9991
Toll free: 877-232-7662 or 877-23A-
ROMA
Fax: 713-896-9500 Fax
scents@onramp.net
www.infrin.com/ifimain.htm

Camden-Grey Essential Oils
7178-A SW 47 Street
Miami, Fla. 33155
Tel: 305-740-3494
Toll free: 877-232-7662

Rainbow Meadow, Inc.
8433 South Avenue, Suite 2
Poland, Ohio 44514
Tel: 330-729-0680
Toll free: 800-207-4047
Fax: 330-729-0685
Andy@rainbowmeadow.com
www.rainbowmeadow.com

Aroma Tech
Attn: John Harrell
130 Industrial Parkway
Somerville, N.J. 08875-6004
Tel: 800-542-7662
Fax: 908-707-1704
mail@aromatec.com
www.aromatec.com

French Color & Chemical
488 Grand Avenue
Englewood, N.J. 07631
Tel: 201-567-6883
Toll free: 800-762-9098
Fax: 201-567-5749
general@frenchcolor.com
www.frenchcolor.com

The Lebermuth Company, Inc.
P.O. Box 4103
South Bend, Ind. 46634
Tel: 800-648-1123
Fax: 800-852-4722
www.lebermuth.com

Robertet, Inc.
125 Bauer Drive
P.O. Box 650
Oakland, N.J. 07436-3190
Tel: 800-631-1182
Fax: 201-337-6863

APPENDIX V
RIT Custom Color Recipes for Powder Dye

AMETHYST
1 pkg Purple
1 Tbsp Wine

APRICOT
1 Tbsp Rose Pink
1 tsp Tangerine

AQUA
1 pkg Royal Blue
1 Tbsp Kelly Green

AQUAMARINE
1 Tbsp Mint Green
1½ tsp Teal

AVOCADO
1 pkg Dark Green
1 pkg Golden Yellow

BEIGE
1 Tbsp Tan
1 tsp Yellow

BITTERSWEET
1 pkg Golden Yellow
1 Tbsp Scarlet

BLUE SPRUCE
1 pkg Royal Blue
1 Tbsp Dark Green

BONE
½ tsp Tan
½ tsp Pearl Grey

BRIGHT NAVY
1 pkg Royal Blue
1 pkg Navy Blue

BURGUNDY
1 pkg Wine
1 pkg Cardinal Red

BURNT ORANGE
1 Tbsp Tangerine
1 Tbsp Tan

CAMEL
1 Tbsp Yellow
1/4 tsp Cocoa Brown

CARAMEL
2 pkg Golden Yellow
1½ tsp Cocoa Brown

CELERY
1 tsp Yellow
1/4 tsp Kelly Green

CHARCOAL GREY
1½ tsp Royal Blue
1½ tsp Black

CHARTREUSE
1 pkg Yellow
1 tsp Kelly Green

CHERRY RED
1 pkg Fuchsia
1 Tbsp Scarlet

CHESTNUT BROWN
2 pkg Cocoa Brown
2 pkg Tangerine

CORAL
1 pkg Rose Pink
2 tsp Tangerine

CRANBERRY RED
1 pkg Scarlet
1 Tbsp Wine

DARK DENIM
2 pkg Navy Blue
1 Tbsp Black

DUSTY ROSE
1 Tbsp Mauve
1 tsp Tan

EGGSHELL
1 tsp Tan
1 tsp Yellow

FLESH
1 tsp Tan
1 tsp Peach

FOREST GREEN
2 pkg Dark Green
1 pkg Yellow

GOLD
1 pkg Golden Yellow
1½ tsp Tan

GRAPE
1 Tbsp Wine
1 Tbsp Purple

HUNTER GREEN
2 pkg Royal Blue
2 pkg Kelly Green

IVORY
½ tsp Tan
½ tsp Yellow

CHAMPAGNE
2 tsp Tan
1/4 tsp Yellow

JADE GREEN
2 pkg Teal
1 pkg Yellow

KHAKI GREEN
1 pkg Tan
1/4 tsp Dark Green

PAPRIKA
1 pkg Golden Yellow
1 Tbsp Scarlet

KHAKI TAN
1 pkg Tan
2 tsp Pearl Grey

PINK
1½ tsp Rose Pink
½ tsp Yellow

LILAC
1 Tbsp Mauve
1 tsp Purple

PLUM
1 pkg Navy
1 Tbsp Wine

LIGHT BLUE
1 Tbsp Evening Blue

RUST
1 pkg Tangerine
1 Tbsp Cocoa Brown

LIGHT TURQUOISE
2 tsp Royal Blue
2 tsp Kelly Green

SAGE GREEN
1 pkg Pearl Grey
1 Tbsp Sea Foam Green

LIME GREEN
2 pkg Yellow
1 pkg Kelly Green

SEA CORAL
1 pkg Rose Pink
1½ tsp Tangerine

OR
1 pkg Yellow
1½ tsp Scarlet

LIGHT GREEN
2 tsp Kelly Green

MAGENTA
1 pkg Fuchsia
2 tsp Wine

MARINE BLUE
1 pkg Royal Blue
1 tsp Purple

SHOCKING PINK
1 pkg Rose Pink
1½ tsp Fuchsia

MAROON
2 pkg Wine
2 tsp Dark Brown

SHRIMP PINK
1 pkg Rose Pink
1 tsp Tangerine

MISTY LAVENDER
1 pkg Evening Blue
1 Tbsp Mauve

SOFT RASPBERRY
1½ tsp Cardinal Red
1 tsp Fuchsia

MOSS GREEN
1 pkg Golden Yellow
1 Tbsp Dark Green
2 tsp Tangerine

SPICE BROWN
1 pkg Cocoa Brown
1 Tbsp Tangerine

MUSTARD
2 pkg Golden Yellow
1 pkg Tan

TEAL BLUE
1 pkg Royal Blue
1½ tsp Kelly Green

OLD ECRU
1 Tbsp Yellow
1½ tsp Tan
1½ tsp Peach

TEAL GREEN
1½ pkg Kelly Green
1 Tbsp Royal Blue

OLIVE DRAB
1 pkg Dark Green
1 Tbsp Dark Brown

TIGER LILY
1 pkg Tangerine
1 Tbsp Rose Pink

ORANGE
1 pkg Golden Yellow
2 tsp Scarlet

GLOSSARY

Appliqué—The technique of adding decorations to the surface of a candle. The appliqué may be a decorative wax design, fabric, or metal decorations, such as gold leaf.

Auto-ignition point–The temperature at which a vapor/air mixture will self-ignite and maintain combustion (remain lit). (I.e. the temperature that will create and keep a flame, without a spark or another flame igniting it.)

Bayberry–A wax made up primarily of lauric, myristic, and palmitic acid esters.

Beeswax—Wax produced by ordinary honeybees for the construction of their combs—where they store honey and lay eggs. Beeswax is obtained during the harvesting of excess honey (honey not needed to sustain the life and vigor of the colony). Beeswax is high melting, sticky, and burns with a beautiful, sweet aroma. Chemically, it consists mainly of wax esters of 26 to 32-carbon fatty alcohols and 24 to 32-carbon fatty acids.

Burn rate—The rate at which a candle burns, usually expressed in grams per hour.

Candelilla—A hard vegetable wax composed of 50-60% hydrocarbons, 30-35% wax esters, and 15-20% fatty acids and alcohols.

Carnauba—The hardest and highest melting vegetable wax, it is composed of 50-60% hydrocarbons, 30-35% wax esters, and 15-20% fatty acids and alcohols. Carnauba wax consists mostly (70-85%) of hydroxylated unsaturated 12-carbon fatty acids and a 30-carbon fatty alcohol (Myricyl ceretate). The flash point is 570 F (310 C).

Clear crystals—Polymer beads added to wax to increase the transparency of the candle. In actuality, these polymers usually contribute hardness and extended burn times while maintaining the normal translucency of paraffins. They do not make a clear wax.

Combustion zone—The zone within a candle where the wax vapors actually combine with oxygen.

Congealing point—The temperature at which a liquid ceases to flow or solidifies when cooled.

Container candle—A candle formed in a container that is designed to hold the candle during burning. Container candles are usually designed to burn the entire wax content of the container.

Container fill—A ready-to-use blended wax designed for containers. It is usually low melting (about 120-125 F) and may have other additives as well to enhance the size of the melt pool, etc.

Crater(ing)—A depression left in the candle due to shrinkage of the wax on cooling; also called a vortex.

Crystal—The three-dimensional, internal structure (atomic, ionic, or molecular) of the wax.

Crystal matrix—The system of interconnected cells that form the crystal.

Dewaxing—A process for separating various wax fractions from petroleum where a solvent is added to the petroleum fraction and the temperature is then reduced until the waxes separate as a solid phase. Dewaxing of a distilled petroleum fraction ordinarily produces normal paraffin waxes while dewaxing of the residue (the fraction not distilled or not distillable) produces microcrystalline waxes.

Dip tank—A metal container holding molten wax for the purpose of dipping (making) tapers or for overdipping.

Dye chip (or block)—A semi-concentrated form of dye that is dissolved in wax, meant to color from 1-10 pounds of wax, depending on the source.

Essential oil—A fragrant, water-insoluble, oily liquid produced either by cold pressing citrus rinds or by the steam distillation of volatiles from herbs and flowers.

Fantasy candle—Any sort of nontraditional decorative candle, such as types of sand candles, fanciful molded or sculpted shapes, etc.

Fischer-Tropsch—A process whereby paraffins are produced from carbon monoxide and hydrogen.

Flash Point—The lowest temperature where wax vapors will remain lit.

Fragrance loading—The amount of fragrance added, often expressed as a percent.

Fragrance evolution—Odor; giving off odor.

Fragrance oil—Any blended, proprietary fragrance designed to scent candles, potpourri, etc.

Free radicals—Highly reactive groups of atoms; they tend to react quickly with most molecules, often causing degradation such as loss of color or metal rusting.

Gel candle—A clear container candle made from mineral oil and a polymeric gelling agent. The mineral oil gel will melt when heated but form a soft-to-firm gel when cooled. Most candle gel is purchased ready to use from a supplier.

Gloss coating—A polymer coating that is applied to a candle to produce a glossy finish, usually a high gloss. Various gloss coats may be solvent based or water based and are often acrylic polymers. Some gloss coatings will ignite on use and are thus designed solely for decorative purposes.

Gloss crystals—Any type of polymer that tends to increase the gloss and luster of a wax blend. They generally increase both hardness and burn times and may contribute opacity. They will typically make colors more vivid.

Hard tallow—Tallow (beef fat) that has been hydrogenated (chemically modified) to transform the oleic acid into stearic acid, thus producing a much harder, more stable, higher melting material.

Hurricane candle—A candle shell meant to surround a smaller, interior candle such as a votive. "Hurricane" indicates that it will shield the burning candle from the wind.

Hydrocarbon—A molecule consisting of carbon and hydrogen atoms.

Hydrosol—The scented water, such as rose water, produced during the production of essential oils.

Interlayer adhesion—The ability of two different wax layers to stick together.

Kemamide(s)—Any one of several fatty acid amides used as a release additive or release wax.

Layered candle—Any candle consisting of more than one color, in layers.

Liquid capacity—Volume; the amount of a liquid required to fill an object.

Melting point—The temperature at which the wax turns liquid (melts). Also called congealing point, or the temperature at which a wax starts to turn back into a solid.

Melt pool—The pool of molten wax that is formed by the heat generated from the flame of a candle. The wax from the melt pool flows up the wick to the combustion zone.

Melt viscosity—Viscosity (thickness or ability to flow) of molten wax.

Micro or microcrystalline wax—One of several types of paraffin waxes that forms small flexible crystals when it solidifies. Micros ordinarily have a greater affinity for oil than regular paraffins. Physical properties range from soft and sticky to very hard. These waxes are characterized by a branched chain and cyclic hydrocarbon content. Micros contain roughly 30 to 75 carbon atoms per chain and are often branched or cyclic in structure.

Mold release—A material that makes it easier to remove a poured candle from a mold. Mold release can be an additive, such as stearic acid; but it usually refers to a silicone spray that is sprayed onto the inside of the mold before pouring the wax.

Mottling—Formation of visible crystals with the appearance of snowflakes or starbursts.

Mottling agent—A liquid or solid additive, which is added to paraffin to produce a mottled or starburst surface effect. Liquid additive, usually mineral oil, is typically added at a level of 2-3%. The solid agents may be used at levels of 4% or higher. The exact composition of the solid agents is unknown except to the suppliers, but based on the physical and safety data, it is likely that they are mixtures of fatty alcohols (probably palmityl and stearyl alcohols).

Mold—Any container used to form a candle by pouring molten wax inside the container.

Mold sealer—A compound that is used to protect a wick and prevent the escape of molten wax from the mold. It is usually a tacky rubber-like substance. Florists putty or Mortite rope caulk may often be substituted for specific mold sealers.

Montan—The wax component of montan is a mixture of long chain (C24-C30) esters (62-68 wt %), long-chain acids (22-26 wt %), and long chain alcohols, ketones, and hydrocarbons (7-15 wt %).

Mordant—A complex solution of salts that are impregnated into wicking to control burn rates and enhance clean burning. Mordanting and braiding meant that the wick tip now fell into the outer zones of the flame where it was consumed, rather than charring and fouling the candle, unless it was constantly trimmed. Previously a candle would require trimming roughly every thirty minutes to assure good-burning performance.

Needle penetration—A measure of the hardness of wax. The depth, under specific conditions (temperature, applied force), that a needle will penetrate into a piece of wax. The higher the value, the softer the wax.

Normal paraffins—Most common candle waxes consist of normal paraffins. Chemically they are hydrocarbons in which the carbon atoms are all bonded, one to another, in a straight line.

Opacity—The property of not being transparent; completely preventing light from passing through.

Overdipping—The process of dipping an otherwise complete candle into molten wax to lay down additional layers on the surface. This technique can be used to apply a clear protective wax coating or to add new colored layers for special color effects (such as dip and carve).

Oxidation—The process of combining with oxygen. Combustion is an oxidation process where a material such as wax combines with oxygen to form carbon dioxide and water.

Petroleum jelly—A soft, low-melting paraffin used to reduce the melting point of waxes for container blends. A well-known consumer brand is Vaseline brand petroleum jelly. It is sometimes called petrolatum or petro.

Paraffin—A residue from oil distillation. A waxy hydrocarbon prepared by dewaxing petroleum distillates. Chemically, paraffins are fully saturated hydrocarbons.

Pillar candle—A candle designed to be freestanding, not needing a candleholder. Pillars may be square, round, conical, or other more complicated shapes.

Plastic additive—Any of a series of polymeric materials which can be added to paraffin to improve the visual or handling properties of a candle. Gloss or translucent additives are types of plastic additives.

Polyethylene—A polymer made from ethylene or having a repeating 2-carbon segment along the chain(s). Polyethylenes (such as waxes) may be linear or branched, depending on how they are produced.

Polymer—May be used to increase properties such as melting point, burn time, and hardness, and to reduce the tendency to crack. In general, useful polymers need to melt around the range of the wax to which they are added. Chemically a polymer is a long, usually high molecular weight material composed of repeating units (monomers). Polymers can be hydrocarbons, polyesters, polyamides, or materials with mixed functionality.

Pour temperature—The temperature where the wax is fluid enough to pour.

Priming—The practice of saturating a wick with paraffin before using it to form a candle. Priming replaces most of the trapped air within the wick with paraffin and thus produces more even delivery of molten wax and more even burning in the candle.

Proteinaceous—Containing protein (animal tissue) or its degradation products.

Release wax—Neither a wax nor a paraffin, these products are usually fatty acid amides that form a single layer of oil on the candle surface, facilitating separation of the candle from the mold.

Repouring—The process of refilling a candle mold after the initial cooling and shrinking of the wax. The shrinkage causes a depression or crater which must be refilled.

ROE—Rosemary oil (or oleoresin extract), a natural antioxidant extracted from the herb rosemary.

Shock crystallization—Rapid induced crystal formation which usually results in very small crystals and, in the case of candle wax, may cause fracturing.

Shrinkage—Waxes expand (increase in volume) when they are heated and liquefied, and then they shrink back (decrease to the original volume) when cooled and allowed to solidify. This shrinkage usually causes a depression or crater in the molded candle, which must be refilled with wax (repouring).

Spermaceti wax—Taken from the head cavity of the sperm whale, it is primarily a wax ester, cetyl palmitate.

Stearic acid—An 18-carbon fatty acid, which is one of the major components of tallow (along with oleic acid, both esterified with glycerin).

Stearin—Used to increase the melting point of waxes, assist in mold release, increase opacity, and to increase the burn time. Chemically, it is the solid fatty acids produced from the splitting (hydrolysis) of tallow or hard vegetable oils. It may refer to relatively pure stearic acid or a blend of stearic and palmitic acids.

Tab—A small, flat metal device that serves to keep the wick from falling over into the wax or onto the side of the container.

Tacky wax—A sticky microcrystalline wax used for attaching sculpted wax ornamentation to a candle or to enhance bonding between layers in dipped or layered candles.

Tallow—The hard fat taken from around the kidneys of cattle, sheep, and goats. It consists primarily of esters of glycerin with stearic, oleic, and palmitic acids.

Taper—A long thin candle formed by dipping a wick into a container of molten wax, usually held just above its melting point.

Tjanting—The use of a device designed for the application of molten wax. The tjanter is used in making pysanky (Russian Easter eggs) and batik. The device can be used to apply decorative drops or lines of wax to the surface of a candle.

Triglyceride—An ester of a fatty acid and glycerin; fats and oils are triglycerides.

Unmolding—Removing from a mold, as in sliding a candle from a mold.

Viscosity—The measure of thickness or ease of pouring. Water has low viscosity, chocolate syrup has higher viscosity, blackstrap molasses has an even higher viscosity, and the viscosity of set gelatin (think of that kid-favorite dessert) is extremely high and quite similar to the viscosity of candle gel.

Volatiles—Materials that evaporate easily and, in candles, usually produce a fragrance.

Votive candle—A candle molded like a pillar, which is intended to be placed in a small container as it burns. These candles are essentially container candles made outside the container. In many cases the votives are actually formed in the container and may be large enough to burn for a week.

Vybar—Added to candles to increase the amount of fragrance oil they are able to contain without mottling or forcing the oil out of the candle upon solidification. Chemically, Vybars are trademarked polyethylenes that are highly branched hydrocarbons, polymers of ethylene, which disrupt the neat, regular orientation of the highly linear paraffin chains. At least one chemical source indicates that the Vybars are actually very specific types of microcrystalline waxes.

Wick—A piece of braided material, usually cotton, which is designed to transfer the molten wax from the candle body (melt pool) to the combustion zone (flame). Wicks are usually soaked in a mordant to enhance burning characteristics.

*I*NDEX

Candle Creations
Ideas for Decoration and Display
by Vivian Peritts
Learn how to quickly and inexpensively change store-bought candles into treasures for your home by using techniques such as adding color, painting, gradation, whipping, softening and twisting. With step-by-step instructions and more than 200 illustrative photographs, you'll be able to recreate the more than 100 beautiful projects with ease.

Softcover • 8-1/4 x 10-7/8 • 128 pages
200+ color photos
Item# CCIE • $21.95

Naturally Creative Candles
by Letty Oates
This unique art form is brought to vivid life as author Letty Oates demonstrates the immense potential of numerous natural materials in making and decorating different candles. More than 250 sharp photos reveal the results of creative candlemaking.

Softcover • 8-1/2 x 11 • 128 pages
250 color photos
Item# NACC • $19.95

Forever Flowers
A Flower Lover's Guide to Selecting, Pressing, and Designing
by Bernice Peitzer
This all-in-one resource includes foolproof methods for sowing, growing, gathering, pressing, storing, and designing and creating with flowers. Provides dozens of projects and ideas for beautiful, functional accents you can keep yourself or give as one-of-a-kind gifts, including pictures, candles, jewelry, bottles, and stationery. Features step-by-step instructions, lavish full-color photos, and tried-and-true tips and techniques.

Softcover • 8-1/4 x 10-7/8 • 128 pages
100 color photos
Item# PRFLO • $21.95

Essentially Soap
The Elegant Art of Handmade Soap Making, Scenting, Coloring, & Shaping
by Dr. Robert S. McDaniel
Make "custom-made" soap with just the right scent, emollients, and eye-appeal. With Dr. Robert McDaniel's simple instructions and numerous recipes, you can make soap to match your decor, soothe your jangled nerves at the end of a hectic day, or energize you in the morning. McDaniel teaches you how to work with fragrances, skin treatments, colors, and shapes and discusses the aromatherapy benefits associated with many essential oils.

Softcover • 8-1/4 x 10-7/8 • 128 pages
100 color photos
Item# SOAP • $19.95

krause publications
since 1952
700 East State Street • Iola, WI 54990-0001
715/445-2214 • FAX: 715/445-4087 • www.krause.com

To order or for a FREE all-product catalog call 800-258-0929 **Offer CRB1**

Shipping & Handling: $4.00 first book, $2.00 each additional.
Non-US addresses $20.95 first book, $5.95 each additional.

Sales Tax: CA, IA, IL, PA, TN, VA, WI residents please add appropriate sales tax.

Creative Ideas to Inspire You

Halloween Crafts
Eerily Elegant Décor
by Kasey Rogers & Mark Wood

Learn how to make unique, vintage looking crafts, such as "Instant Ancestors" (faux gravestones) and scarecrow wreaths, to decorate your home for Halloween. Join Kasey Rogers, "Louise Tate" from the classic television show Bewitched, and Mark Wood as they guide you through these 50 bewitching crafts and party recipes with which to celebrate the holiday. Most projects are quick and simple, requiring not much more than a glue gun, a little sewing and painting.

Softcover • 8-1/4 x 10-7/8 • 128 pages
150 color photos
Item# WTCHC • $19.95

The Good Earth Bath, Beauty & Health Book
by Casey Kellar

In this practical guide to beauty and well-being, you will learn how to make Mother Nature your Fairy Godmother! With remedies and toiletries made with natural, simple formulas and ingredients found in health food, drug, and grocery stores, you can learn how to pamper yourself. The more than 75 formulas-including those for lotions, toothpaste, cough syrup, lip balm, and hair care-will enhance your health and produce spa-quality beauty results.

Softcover • 8-1/4 x 10-7/8 • 112 pages
75 color photos
Item# GEBBH • $19.95

The Complete Guide to Glues & Adhesives
by Nancy Ward & Tammy Young

In 1995, Tammy Young's The Crafter's Guide to Glues took the crafting world by storm. Now, Tammy has teamed up with Nancy Ward for this full-color follow-up that covers everything you need to know about glues and adhesives currently on the market, including their uses and applications for memory crafting, stamping, embossing, and embellishing any surface. Besides presenting the basics, like safety, there are more than 30 quick and easy step-by-step projects.

Softcover • 8-1/4 x 10-7/8 • 144 pages
75 color photos
Item# CGTG2 • $19.95

Wire in Design
Modern Wire Art & Mixed Media
by Barbara A. McGuire

Whether you have an interest in wire's rich past or the desire to explore this creative medium, this is the perfect book for you! Besides giving an overview of how artists have used wire effectively in their art, Barbara A. McGuire will teach you the basics of handling wire and about its unique properties, as well as provide more than 15 projects, including jewelry, functional accessories, and sculptures.

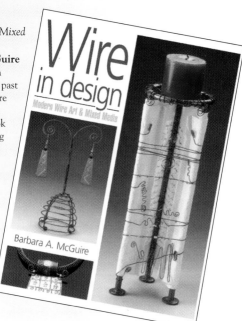

Softcover • 8-1/4 x 10-7/8 • 144 pages
150 color photos
Item# WIDE • $21.95

krause publications
since 1952
700 East State Street • Iola, WI 54990-0001
715/445-2214 • FAX: 715/445-4087   www.krause.com

To order or for a FREE all-product catalog call 800-258-0929 **Offer CRB1**

Shipping & Handling: $4.00 first book, $2.00 each additional.
Non-US addresses $20.95 first book, $5.95 each additional.

Sales Tax: CA, IA, IL, PA, TN, VA, WI residents please add appropriate sales tax.